SCHOOL LIBRARY MEDIA SERIES
Edited by Diane de Cordova Biesel

TODDLER STORYTIME PROGRAMS

by
DIANE BRIGGS

School Library Media Series, No. 2

The Scarecrow Press, Inc.

British Library Cataloguing-in-Publication data available

Library of Congress Cataloging-in-Publication Data

Briggs, Diane.
    Toddler storytime programs / by Diane Briggs.
      p.   cm. — (School library media series ; no. 2)
    Includes bibliographical references and indexes.
    ISBN 0-8108-2777-8 (alk. paper)
    1. Storytelling. 2. Children's stories. 3. Flannelgraphs. 4. Early childhood
education—Activity programs. I. Title. II. Series.
LB1140.35.S76B75   1993
372.64'2—dc20   93-41572

To toddlers everywhere

And to Ken Briggs

with love

for all his support and interest

CONTENTS

EDITOR'S FOREWORD

The School Library Media Series is directed to the school library media specialist, particularly the building-level librarian. The multifaceted role of the librarian as educator, collection developer, curriculum developer, and information specialist is examined. The series includes concise, practical books on topical and current subjects related to programs and services.

Shall I call *Toddler Storytime Programs* by Diane Briggs magically charming or charmingly magic? Arranged around themes understood by toddlers, Part I includes stories, rhymes and activities. Both traditional and original rhymes are used in the fingerplays. Part II includes flannel board activities. Realistic advise throughout the book shows the author's extensive experience with toddlers.

Here's to storytimes that are lots of fun!

Diane de Cordova Biesel
Series Editor

PREFACE

Toddler Storytime Programs is a sourcebook for librarians, teachers, and anyone else who works with toddlers. These are the program ideas that I have put together and used successfully during the course of my work as a children's librarian and storyteller. You may prefer to reproduce the programs just as they are described. But most likely, many of you will mix and match the ideas presented here with favorite activities of your own.

Part I of this book contains twenty-five theme programs with book suggestions, fingerplays, puppetry ideas, songs, games, activities, and crafts. Part II features flannel board activities with full-size reproducible patterns. This book also contains a music appendix with guitar chords, an index to authors and titles, and an index to fingerplays.

I would like to thank all the supportive librarians and storytellers with whom I've shared ideas. My sincere thanks go to Jan Barclay, Lisa Bouchard, Joni Goldberg, Polly Hartman, Peg Lewis and Beverly Provost. I'd also like to thank Anne Brew for permission to use her song "Storytime is Over Now," Fay Lewis for her tip on how to make sturdy flannel board figures, and Kathy Liebman for doing the typing. Finally, my special thanks and love go to Mom, Dad, and Helen for their moral support and interest.

I hope the material contained in this book will help you to present effective and entertaining programs for toddlers. Enjoy!

INTRODUCTION

THE BENEFITS OF TODDLER STORYTIMES

Storytime programs can be wonderful experiences for toddlers[1] and their parents. During storytime, toddlers learn to participate in games, fingerplays, rhymes, and songs and are exposed to quality children's literature and art in picture books. The storytime experience helps to stimulate cognitive development and is one of the first steps towards a love of libraries, books, and reading.

Much of the research done in the field of early childhood development has shown that toddlerhood is a crucial time for learning. Language and cognitive skills are developing at an amazing rate. In his book *From Two to Five* Kornei Chukovsky writes, "It seems to me that, beginning with the age of two, every child becomes for a short time a linguistic genius.... If an adult had to master so many grammatical rules within so short a time, his head would surely burst."[2] It is up to us as educators and parents to provide toddlers with as many learning opportunities as possible during this important developmental stage.

Toddler storytimes can be a great help to parents. These programs provide an opportunity for parents, as their child's best teachers, to gather ideas for more learning experiences at home. Stories, fingerplays, songs, and games, repeated at home, all add to a child's cognitive development. Parents will also enjoy opportunities to meet other parents of toddlers to exchange notes, give support, and develop friendships.

Finally, one of the best benefits of toddler storytimes is that they are a lot of fun!

PLANNING STORYTIMES FOR TODDLERS

Toddler storytimes require careful planning. The books you choose should be short with simple plots and large, colorful, well-defined illustrations. Use a variety of media. Act out a story or rhyme with puppets. Tell flannel board stories and include several fingerplays, action rhymes, and songs. Remember to keep all selections short and use physical activities, such as fingerplays or creative drama, frequently throughout a program. Physical activities help to release energy, refocus attention, and help with transitions between stories.

The length of a toddler program should be approximately twenty minutes. If you are including a craft activity, a program may last up to forty-five minutes.

---

1. The programs in this book are designed for toddlers between the ages of twenty-two months and three years. However, many of the activities included here can be used successfully with younger or older children.

2. Kornei Chukovsky, *From Two to Five*, trans. and edited by Miriam Morton (Berkeley: University of California Press), 1966.

BOOKS

When selecting books for toddlers consider the following points.

1. Be sure the content of the book is familiar to toddlers. Select themes that are part of a toddler's world.

2. The pictures should be large, colorful, and well-defined against their backgrounds. Look for clear, uncluttered illustrations.

3. Plots should be simple and linear. Choose stories that are short with no more than three or four characters. Toddlers will enjoy books without plots as well.

4. Choose stories that are repetitive in their words or actions. Cumulative stories such as *Brown Bear, Brown Bear, What Do You See?* by Bill Martin are good choices also.

5. Toddlers will enjoy participating while you read noisy books like Sandra Boynton's *Moo Baa La La La,* Pat Hutchin's *Goodnight Owl,* or *Who Said Meow?* by Maria Polushkin.

6. Look for books that lead into other activities such as fingerplays, songs, or creative dramatics.

FINGERPLAYS AND ACTION RHYMES

Fingerplays and action rhymes are great attention getters and they are an ideal way to start a story program. In some ways, they are the glue that holds a toddler program together. They are especially helpful as transitions between stories. Many fingerplays are wonderful rhymes that have been passed down through the generations. Therefore, you are not just doing fingerplays. You are passing on the rich tradition of children's folklore. If you have a favorite fingerplay, use it often. Toddlers enjoy repeating familiar favorites.

Avoid small finger motions. Toddlers have not yet developed the fine motor skills necessary to do them. Instead, use the arms, legs, and body and create larger motions to go with your favorite rhymes.

Lastly, toddlers should never be forced to do fingerplays. Many toddlers will simply want to watch and that's fine. It's important that parents join in on the fingerplays. This makes it more likely their toddlers will too.

PUPPETS

Puppets are indispensable helpmates for storytellers and toddlers love them. Puppets, in a nonthreatening way, allow toddlers to get close to the storyteller. They are perfect for saying hello and introducing a storytime theme. You may want to use them to sing a song, act out a rhyme, or tell a story.

A soft, cuddly puppet has a very important role to play when storytime is over. When it's time to say good-bye, toddlers need time to absorb what has happened during storytime and prepare themselves to leave. A soft, furry puppet to hug and kiss helps with this transition in the best way possible.

THE MAGIC OF MUSIC

Toddlers love music. When your group gets restless or their attention needs focusing, a song will draw them in. If you are doing a weekly storytime, pick out a greeting song to use every time. This establishes a routine and helps the toddlers to feel secure. Use a puppet to sing the song or play it on an autoharp or guitar. You may want to use a "good morning" song or, perhaps, a friendship song. A traditional children's folksong called "The More We Get Together" is one that works well. This song can be found in *The Raffi Singable Songbook*[3] and in many other collections of children's folksongs.

If you play a musical instrument, use it in your storytime. If you don't play an instrument, consider the autoharp. It's easy to learn and works well for storytimes. If you don't want to bother with an instrument, that's fine. Singing a cappella is wonderful too. If you feel you are not "musical" and can't carry a tune, just remember that the toddlers won't care. If you still feel uncomfortable singing, play cassette tapes and sing along. Make sure parents are joining in too!

Finally, it's nice to have a closing song. This is one that I use.

Storytime is Over Now

(Tune: "London Bridge"; Words: Anne Brew)

Storytime is over now, over now,
over now.
Storytime is over now, see you
next time.

THE FLANNEL BOARD

For toddlers the flannel board can be magical. It is intriguing to them how those little people and animals stick to the board with just a touch of the finger. Flannel board stories, songs, and poems hold a toddler's attention very effectively. Be sure to include at least one flannel board presentation per storytime. Because flannel board activities are so essential to successful toddler storytimes, Part II of this book is devoted to this medium of storytelling.

CRAFT ACTIVITIES

A craft activity is a wonderful way to end a toddler program and provides something for the toddlers to take home. Although you may not be able to provide a craft for every program you do, the crafts in this book are designed with simplicity and time limitations in mind.

Things to consider before deciding on a craft:

* Keep the craft simple. Toddlers have trouble gluing on small items such as craft eyes or sequins. They might even decide to eat them. Keep the pieces fairly large.

* Use glue sticks to avoid messes on clothing, in hair, or elsewhere.

---

3. Raffi, *The Raffi Singable Songbook* (New York: Crown), 1987.

* Provide interesting materials to work with that the toddlers may not have experienced before. For example: feathers, pom-poms, or shiny paper.

PARTICIPATION OF PARENTS OR CAREGIVERS

Toddlers need to be accompanied by a parent or caregiver during a story program. Most people would assume this, but it is a good idea to include this information in a special flyer that can be distributed to parents and caregivers during storytime registration.

Some other things that parents or caregivers should know are:

1. Toddlers need to be prepared for storytime. Talk to your toddler about what will happen during storytime. It will help your child to feel more secure upon entering this new situation.

2. Adults should participate in activities such as fingerplays, rhymes, and songs. This will make your toddler more likely to join in and is a lot more fun for everyone.

3. Take time to talk with the storyteller and learn some of the fingerplays and songs so they can be repeated at home.

4. If possible, older children should not attend toddler storytimes. This should be a special time for parents and toddlers to focus on the storytime experience.

STORYTIME REGISTRATION

The programs in this book may be used for small groups (10-15) or larger groups (30-40). The type of the programs you put on will depend on your facilities and staff. It is a good idea to require that parents preregister their children for storytime programs. This ensures that the program will be taken seriously and attendance will be good. Keep a good record of your program statistics. A compilation of the number of programs, the attendance, and the time involved, may prove very helpful for budget justification.

PART I: STORYTIME PROGRAMS FOR TODDLERS

GONE FISHING

BOOKS

Who Sank the Boat? by Pamela Allen. New York: Coward-McCann, 1982.

Guess who causes the boat to sink when five funny animals of all sizes decide to go for a row.

Just Like Daddy by Frank Asch. Englewood Cliffs, NJ: Prentice-Hall, 1981.

A young bear does everything just like his daddy and then one day they go fishing.

FINGERPLAYS/ACTION RHYMES

Five Little Fishes

Five little fishes swimming in a pool
    (hold up five fingers)

First one said, "This pool is cool."
    (hug self and shiver)

Second one said, "This pool is deep."
    (point downward)

Third one said, "I think I'll sleep."
    (close eyes and rest head on hands)

Fourth one said, "Let's swim and dip."
    (do swimming and dipping motions)

Fifth one said, "I see a ship."
    (look into distance with hand shading eyes)

The fisherman's line went splish, splish, splash,
and away the five little fishes dashed.
    (make fishing pole motions and
    quickly put hands behind back)

Once I Caught a Fish Alive

One, two, three, four, five!
    (point to fingers)

Once I caught a fish alive.
Six, seven, eight, nine, ten!
    (point to fingers)

Then I let it go again.
Why did I let it go?
Because it bit my finger so!
Which finger did it bite?
The little finger on the right.
(point to little finger on right hand)
- *Mother Goose*

GAME

Make several small fish out of poster board or heavy paper (at least one for each child). Glue inexpensive magnets to the back of each one. Place the fish in a child's wading pool. Make fishing poles out of drinking straws and yarn. Attach large paper clips to the ends of the pieces of yarn. The toddlers will love going "fishing" in the "pond." Allow each child to take their pole and one fish home.

MUSIC

All the Fish are Swimming in the Water

(For melody see Music Appendix, Song 1)

All the fish are swimming in the water
swimming in the water
swimming in the water
All the fish are swimming in the water
On this sunny, sunny, day!

FLANNEL BOARD ACTIVITY

My Little Fish

(See pages 82-85 for poem and patterns)

CRAFT

Underwater Fish Scene

Let the toddlers glue cellophane strips (seaweed) and fish cut-outs to construction paper and create a beautiful underwater fish scene.

Supplies Needed:

Construction paper
Strips of colored cellophane
Small fish cut-outs
Crayons
Glue sticks

MORE BOOKS OF INTEREST

Ehlert, Lois   *Fish Eyes*
Gomi, Taro   *Where's the Fish*
Lionni, Leo   *Swimmy*
Mac Carthy, Patricia   *Ocean Parade: a
                                              Counting Book*
Raffi   *Baby Beluga*
Seuss, Dr.   *McElligot's Pool*

SPRING FLING

BOOKS

The Chick and the Duckling by Mirra Ginsburg, illus. by Jose and Ariane Aruego. New York: Macmillan, 1982.

"Me too!" says the chick as he follows the duckling around. The chick wants to do everything his friend does. Then the duckling decides to go for a swim.

Tom and Pippo in the Garden by Helen Oxenbury. New York: Macmillan, 1988.

Tom has fun playing in the garden with his toy monkey and wheelbarrow.

FINGERPLAYS/ACTION RHYMES

During Spring

During spring it often showers,
    (flutter fingers)

Or the sun shines for many hours.
    (form circle in the air with arms)

Both are good for the flowers
    (cup hands and extend arms upward)

Once I Saw a Bunny

Once I saw a bunny
    (hold up two fingers)

And a green, green cabbage head
    (hold up fist)

I think I'll have some cabbage
The little bunny said
So he nibbled and he nibbled
    (pretend to nibble with fingers)

And he perked up his ears to say
    (hold up fingers)

"I think it's time to be hopping on my way"
    (hop fingers away and put them behind
    back)

MUSIC

Little Rabbit Foo-Foo

(This song can be dramatized with puppets or done as a fingerplay)

(For melody and additional verses see Music Appendix, Song 2)

Little Rabbit Foo-Foo, Hopping through the forest
Scooping up the field mice, And bopping them on the head.

Down came the Good Fairy, And she said--

Little Rabbit Foo-Foo, I don't like your attitude
Scooping up the field mice, And bopping them on the head.

I'll give you three chances,
And if you don't behave,
I'll turn you into a goon.
The next day--.

FLANNEL BOARD ACTIVITY

Some Things That Spring Brings

(See pages 86-89 for poem and patterns)

CRAFT

Little Rabbit Foo-Foo Puppet

Glue pre-cut construction paper pieces onto toilet paper roll to create a rabbit puppet. Glue on a cotton ball tail.

Supplies Needed:

Toilet paper rolls painted white
Construction paper
Cotton balls
Glue sticks

(see illustration next page)

MORE BOOKS OF INTEREST

Dabcovich, Lydia	*Sleepy Bear*
Krauss, Ruth	*The Carrot Seed*
Rockwell, Anne	*My Spring Robin*
Wells, Rosemary	*Forest of Dreams*
Williams, Garth	*The Chicken Book*
Ziefert, Harriet	*New Boots For Spring*
Zolotow, Charlotte	*In My Garden*

TODDLER TRIATHLON

BOOKS

Calico Cat's Exercise Book by Donald Charles. Chicago: Childrens Press, 1982.

Calico Cat leads a class of mice through an exercise routine.

Get Set! Go! by Shigeo Watanabe, illus. by Yasuo Ohtomo. New York: Philomel, 1980.

Bear shows great determination on his run through an obstacle race.

FINGERPLAYS AND ACTION RHYMES

We Can Jump

We can jump, jump, jump
We can hop, hop, hop
We can clap, clap, clap
We can stop, stop, stop
We can stretch up both our arms
We can reach and touch our toes
We can bend our knees a little bit
And sit down slow

Bouncy Ball

Here is a big round bouncy ball!
I bounce it 1 - 2 - 3
Here is a ball for throwing
I catch it; watch and see!
Here is a ball for rolling
Please roll it back to me

(Use a large Nerf ball to perform the activities
in the rhyme. Give each toddler a turn at
rolling the ball back to you.)

MUSIC

Head, Shoulders, Knees, and Toes

(For melody see Music Appendix, Song 3)

Head and shoulders, knees, and toes, knees and toes
Head and shoulders, knees, and toes, knees and toes
Eyes and ears and mouth and nose
Head and shoulders, knees and toes, knees and toes

FLANNEL BOARD ACTIVITY

The Tortoise and the Hare

(See pages 90-92 for story and patterns)

ACTIVITIES

Set up an athletic course with several fun and interesting stations. Here are some suggestions.

1. Traffic cones to run around
2. Large boxes to climb through
3. Nerf balls to toss in baskets
4. A rope to jump over (1" from ground)
5. Step stools to climb over
6. Small Frisbees to toss (discus)

Before sending the toddlers and their parents through the athletic course, you may want to do some warm-ups with them. You can ask them to balance on tip-toes, hop on one foot, balance on one leg, or any other motions that come to mind.

When you are ready to send them through the athletic course, let them know that they may go through it more than once, but they must go to the end of the line each time. When each child crosses the finish line, be sure someone is there to cheer them on. After completing the athletic course, toddlers and parents may report to a table to receive a gold medal. (To make medals, cover small poster board circles with gold foil and attach a ribbon.)

During the activities you may want to play background music. Some suggestions are "Theme From Chariots of Fire" or "Olympic Fanfare and Theme."[4]

MORE BOOKS OF INTEREST

Carlson, Nancy	*Bunnies and Their Sports*
Galdone, Paul	*The Tortoise and the Hare*
Kessler, Leonard P.	*On Your Mark, Get Set, Go!*
Ormerod, Jan	*Bend and Stretch*
Moncute, Jane	*Healthkins Exercise!*

---

[4] "Theme from Chariots of Fire," *Chariots of Fire: Music from the Original Soundtrack,* composed and performed by Vangelis. Polydor, cassette no. 825384-4.

"Olympic Fanfare and Theme," *By Request.... The Best of John Williams and the Boston Pops Orchestra,* composed by John Williams. Philip, cassette no. 420178-4.

TUB TIME

BOOKS

I Can Take a Bath by Shigeo Watanabe, illus. By Yasuo Ohtomo. New York: Philomel Books, 1987.

Bear doesn't want to take a bath until he realizes how much fun it is.

Oh, My Baby Bear! by Audrey Wood. San Diego: Harcourt Brace Jovanovich, 1990.

Baby bear discovers he is old enough to do all kinds of things for himself, including taking a bath.

FINGERPLAYS/ACTION RHYMES

Bubbles

This is the way we blow our bubbles
Blow, blow, blow
      (hold out imaginary bubble wand and blow)

This is the way we break our bubbles
Oh! Oh! Oh!
      (clap hands together)

Bath Time

(Tune: "Frere Jacques")

It is bath time, it is bath time
Get in the tub, get in the tub.
      (pretend to step into a tub)

Wash your knees and elbows,
Toes and ears and now your nose.
      (pretend to wash)

Oh, what fun!
You're all done.

- Diane Briggs

MUSIC

Rub-a-Dub-Dub

(For melody see Music Appendix, Song 4)

Rub-a-dub-dub, three men in a tub
And who do you think they be?
The butcher, the baker, the candlestick maker
And all of them gone to sea.

FLANNEL BOARD ACTIVITY

Marvelous Mud

(See pages 93-95 for story and patterns)

ACTIVITY

Play cassette tapes of bathtime songs[5] while you blow bubbles. To produce lots of bubbles use a giant bubble wand or enlist several volunteers to blow bubbles with smaller wands. The toddlers will have great fun chasing and popping the bubbles.

CRAFT

Create a painting with soap powder finger paint.

Recipe

Mix two parts Ivory Snow laundry soap with one part water.
Add food coloring to create a variety of color choices.

MORE BOOKS OF INTEREST

Graham, Bob	*Bath Time For John*
Hayes, Geoffrey	*Patrick Takes a Bath*
Inkpen, Mick	*One Bear at Bedtime*
Lindgren, Barbro	*Sam's Bath*
McPhail, David	*Andrew's Bath*
Pryor, Ainslie	*Baby Blue Cat and the Dirty Dog Brothers*
Wells, Rosemary	*Max's Bath*

---

[5]. Suggestions:

"Bathtime," *Raffi in Concert with the Rise and Shine Band*, MCA, cassette no. MCAC-10035.

"Rubber Ducky," *Bob's Favorite Street Songs*, A & M Records, no. 10414.

TEDDY BEAR'S PICNIC

BOOKS

Where's My Teddy? by Jez Alborough. Cambridge, MA: Candlewick, 1992.

A little boy and a huge bear search for their lost teddies.

My Old Teddy by Dom Mansell. Cambridge, MA: Candlewick, 1992.

Despite how worn out teddy has become, he is not forgotten even when a new bear comes along.

FINGERPLAYS/ACTION RHYMES

Bear In A Cave

Here is a cave, inside is a bear.
    (hold up fist)

Now he comes out to get some fresh air.
    (move thumb away from fist. The
    thumb represents the bear)

He stays out all summer in sunshine and heat.
He hunts in the forest for berries to eat.
    (spread the fingers of the other hand to
    represent forest. Bear searches between
    fingers for berries)

When snow starts to fall he hurries inside,
    (return thumb to fist)

His warm little cave and there he will hide.
When spring comes again the snow melts away,
And out comes the bear, ready to play.
    (move thumb away from fist)

He stays out all summer in sunshine and heat,
He hunts in the forest for berries to eat.
    (search for berries as before)

Teddy Bear, Teddy Bear

Teddy Bear, Teddy Bear, turn right around,
Teddy Bear, Teddy Bear, touch the ground,
Teddy Bear, Teddy Bear, dance on your toes,
Teddy Bear, Teddy Bear, touch your nose,
Teddy Bear, Teddy Bear, climb the stairs,
Teddy Bear, Teddy Bear, say your prayers,
Teddy Bear, Teddy Bear, turn out the light,
Teddy Bear, Teddy Bear, say good night.
    - American folk rhyme

PUPPETS

My Teddy Bear by Chiyoko Nakatani is the story of a day in the life of a boy and his bear. Use a talking-mouth boy puppet to narrate the story. Have an assistant manipulate the other puppets and props.

Puppets and Props

Boy puppet with a talking mouth
Bear puppet
Toy car
Dog puppet
Bibs for boy and bear
Poster board silhouette of bathtub
Bubble wand (to make bath bubbles)
Clothesline
Bed

MUSIC

The Bear Went Over the Mountain

(Tune: "For He's a Jolly Good Fellow")

The bear went over the mountain,
The bear went over the mountain,
The bear went over the mountain,
To see what he could see.
And all that he could see,
And all that he could see was,
The other side of the mountain,
The other side of the mountain,
The other side of the mountain,
Was all that he could see.

FLANNEL BOARD ACTIVITY

Five Brown Teddies

(See pages 96-97 for poem and patterns)

ACTIVITIES

This program is a lot of fun held outdoors, weather permitting. Provide refreshments or ask the families to bring their own picnic goodies. Be sure to play the song "The Teddy Bear's Picnic" on cassette tape. This song has been recorded by a number of children's musicians. Play the song while having a teddy bear dance.

MORE BOOKS OF INTEREST

Butler, Dorothy *My Brown Bear Barney*
Cartwright, Stephen *Find the Teddy*
Kozikowski, Renate *The Teddy Bear's Picnic*
Lawson, Carole *Teddy Bear, Teddy Bear*
Mack, Stan *Ten Bears in My Bed*
Rosen, Michael *We're Going on a Bear Hunt*
Young, Ruth *Golden Bear*

WON'T YOU BE MY VALENTINE?

BOOKS

I Love My Mommy Because by Laurel Porter-Gaylord, illus. by Ashley Wolff. New York: Dutton, 1991.

Features all the good things mommies do for their children.

Hugs by Alice McLerran, illus. by Mary Morgan. New York: Scholastic, 1993.

All kinds of hugs are described in this warm-hearted book.

FINGERPLAYS/ACTIONS RHYMES

Won't You Be My Valentine?

Won't you "bee" my valentine
    (point to children)

And buzz away with me?
    (pretend to fly)

We'll bumble along together,
Because you're my Honey Bee.
    (blow kisses)

Bzzzzzz!

Valentine in a Box

Valentine in a box sits so still.
    (squat down)

Won't you come out? Yes, I will!
    (jump up)

PUPPETS

Use a talking-mouth hand puppet to say the following rhyme and distribute valentines.

I have valentines to give away,
One for each of you
Come and get one when you may,
Because I love you!
- Diane Briggs

MUSIC

Lavender's Blue

(For melody see Music Appendix, Song 6)

Lavender's blue, dilly, dilly, Lavender's green;
When I am King, dilly, dilly, you shall be Queen.
Who told you so, dilly, dilly, who told you so?
'Twas my own heart, dilly, dilly, that told me so.

FLANNEL BOARD ACTIVITY

Lots of Valentines

(See pages 98-100 for poem and patterns)

CRAFT

Fingers for Legs Valentine Puppet

Cut hearts out of heavy paper or poster board. The small hearts (the heads) may be made with construction paper. Cut two finger holes in the larger heart as shown. Let the toddlers glue on the small heart and pre-cut arms. You may also want to provide doilies, shiny paper, yarn (for hair), or stickers for the toddlers to add to the puppets.

Supplies Needed:

Heavy paper -- red
Construction paper -- pink
Glue sticks
Optional: doilies
    shiny paper
    yarn
    stickers

MORE BOOKS OF INTEREST

Bunting, Eve — *The Valentine Bear*
Flack, Marjorie — *Ask Mr. Bear*
Hillert, Margaret — *I Love You, Dear Dragon*
Hurd, Thacher — *Little Mouse's Big Valentine*
Jewell, Nancy — *Snuggle Bunny*
Porter-Gaylord, Laurel — *I Love My Daddy Because*
Schweninger, Ann — *Valentine Friends*
Zolotow, Charlotte — *Hold My Hand*

RIDIN' IN MY CAR

BOOKS

Mr. Gumpy's Motor Car by John Burningham. New York: Crowell, 1973.

Children and animals of all types pile into a motor car and go for a ride.

Wheels on the Bus by Paul O. Zelinsky. New York: Dutton, 1990.

A wonderful pull-the-tab, sing-along book.

FINGERPLAYS/ACTION RHYMES

I'm a Little Sports Car

I'm a little sports car,
Shiny and yellow.
When I go out driving,
    (make steering motion)

I'm a very happy fellow.

When the rain comes down,
    (flutter fingers downward)

I turn my wipers on.
    (move arms back and forth to indicate wipers)

It's fun to splash through puddles,
    (move around as if driving)

All around the town.

When I see a red light,
I stop on a dime
    (stop moving).

When I see a green light,
I know it's driving time
    (go forward).

Vroom! Vroom!

- Diane Briggs

Wheels on the Bus

The wheels on the bus go 'round and 'round
'round and 'round, 'round and 'round
The wheels on the bus go 'round and 'round
all around the town.
The wipers on the bus go swish, swish, swish...
The horn on the bus goes beep, beep, beep...
The babies on the bus go waa, waa, waa...
The mommies on the bus go shh, shh, shhh...

MUSIC

Down By The Station

(For melody see Music Appendix, Song 7)

Down by the station, early in the morning,
See the little pufferbellies all in a row,
See the engine driver pull the little handle,
Chug, Chug, Puff, Puff! Off we go!

FLANNEL BOARD ACTIVITY

I Saw A Giraffe Drive By

(See pages 101-106 for poem and patterns)

CRAFT

Sports Car

Toddlers will need assistance from parents as they construct the car. When they finish, let them "motor" around the room in their new jalopies. Play car songs on a tape player.

Supplies Needed:

1. A child-sized cardboard box with the top and bottom cut out.
2. Construction paper for taillights, license plates, wheels, and controls.
3. Aluminum foil for headlights.
4. Sturdy paper plates and brads for steering wheels.
5. Glue sticks.

BOOKS TO SHARE AT HOME

Barton, Byron   *Wheels*
Burningham, John   *Slam Bang*
Fowler, Richard   *Cat's Car*
Fowler, Richard   *Mr. Little's Noisy Fire Engine*
Gay, Michael   *Take Me For A Ride*
Hellen, Nancy   *The Bus Stop*
Lindgren, Barbro   *Sam's Car*
Rockwell, Anne   *Cars*

RHYME TIME WITH MOTHER GOOSE

BOOKS

Mary Had A Little Lamb by Sarah Josepha Hale, photo-illus. by Bruce McMillan. New York: Scholastic, 1990.

Photo-illustrations accompany the famous nursery poem/song.

The Three Little Kittens by Lorinda Bryan Cauley. New York: Putnam, 1982.

The familiar verse illustrated with wonderful drawings.

FINGERPLAYS/ACTION RHYMES

Two Little Black Birds

Two little black birds sitting on a hill,
   (hold up index fingers)

One named Jack and one named Jill.
Fly away Jack, fly away Jill,
   (flutter one hand and hide behind back and then
   the other)

Come back Jack, come back Jill.
Two little black birds sitting on a hill.
               - *Mother Goose*

Open and Shut Them

Open and shut them, Open and shut them
   (open and shut hands)

And give a little clap.
Open and shut them, Open and shut them
And put them in your lap.
Creep them, creep them, creep them, creep them,
   (creep fingers up front of body)

Right up to your chin.
Open up your little mouth,
   (open mouth)

But do not let them in!
   (hide hands behind back)

PUPPETS

Many nursery rhymes can be easily pantomimed with puppets. Some suggestions are "Hickory, Dickory, Dock," "Sing a Song of Sixpence," "Little Miss Muffet," "Little Robin Redbreast," or "Humpty Dumpty." "Hey, Diddle, Diddle" is given as an example below.

Hey, Diddle, Diddle

Hey, diddle, diddle!
The cat and the fiddle,
The cow jumped over the moon.
The little dog laughed to see such sport,
And the dish ran away with the spoon.

Puppets and Props

Cat hand puppet with cardboard fiddle attached
Cow stick puppet
Poster board moon
Dog hand puppet
Dish and spoon stick puppets

MUSIC

Little Miss Muffet

(For melody see Music Appendix, Song 8)

Little Miss Muffet
Sat on a tuffet
Eating her curds and whey.
Along came a spider
Who sat down beside her
And frightened Miss Muffet away.

FLANNEL BOARD ACTIVITY

Old Mother Goose

(See pages 107-110 for poem and patterns)

GAME

Sing the first verse of "London Bridge" several times as the children and parents walk under the "bridge" made by two adults. Avoid doing "take the key and lock her up." This may scare some toddlers.

CRAFT

Two Little Black Birds

Cut birds out of construction paper and glue them onto craft sticks. Give the toddlers colorful feathers to glue onto the wings and tails. Paper eyes may also be glued on. The stick puppets may be used to act out the rhyme on page 26.

Supplies Needed:

Black construction paper
Craft sticks
Feathers
Glue sticks

BOOKS TO SHARE AT HOME

Ahlberg, Janet   *Each Peach Pear Plum*
Aylesworth, Jim   *The Cat and the Fiddle and More*
Hague, Michael   *Mother Goose*
Ivimey, John   *Three Blind Mice*
Lobel, Arnold   *Random House Book of Mother*
                                      Goose
Potter, Beatrix   *Beatrix Potter's Nursery Rhyme Book*
Provensen, Alice   *Old Mother Hubbard*

DOWN ON THE FARM

BOOKS

One Red Rooster by Kathleen Sullivan Carroll, illus. Suzette Barbier. Boston: Houghton Mifflin, 1992.

    A rhymed text with large, clear illustrations featuring a variety of noisy farm animals.

Vegetable Garden by Douglas Florian. San Diego: Harcourt Brace Jovanovich, 1992.

    A book depicting all the activities involved in gardening such as planting, hoeing, watering, and watching the garden grow.

FINGERPLAYS/ACTION RHYMES

My Garden

This is my garden
    (hands in front palm up)

I'll rake it with care
    (rake with fingers)

And then some flower seeds,
    (sprinkle seeds)

I'll plant in there
    (pat palm with fingers)

The sun will shine
    (make circle with arms overhead)

And the rain will fall,
    (wiggle fingers downward)

And my garden will blossom
    (make fists, open fingers slowly)

Growing straight and tall
    (reach hands high above head)

The Barnyard

When the farmer's day is done,
In the barnyard, everyone,
Beast and bird politely say,
"Thank you for my food today."
The cow says, "Moo!"
The pigeon, "Coo!"
The lamb says, "Maa!"
The sheep says, "Baa!"
"Quack!" says the duck,

Says the hen, "Cluck, cluck!"
The dog, "Bow wow!"
The cat, "Meow!"
The horse says, "Neigh!"
"I love sweet hay!"
The pig near by
Grunts in his sty.
When the barn is locked up tight,
Then the farmer says, "Goodnight!"
And thanks his animals, every one,
For the work that has been done.

PUPPETS

Create a barnyard scene on an 18" X 24" piece of cardboard. Cut the barn windows and doors so that they open. Cut other small round holes elsewhere. As you sing "Old MacDonald," insert finger puppets of various farm animals through the openings while holding the panel on your lap. The toddlers will be surprised and delighted to see the tiny animals appear.

MUSIC

Down on Grandpa's Farm

(For melody and additional verses see Music Appendix, Song 9)

Oh we're on our way, we're on our way,
On our way to Grandpa's farm.
     (repeat)
Down on Grandpa's farm there is a big brown
cow. Down on Grandpa's farm there is
a big brown cow. The cow, she makes a
sound like this: Moo! Moo! The cow,
she makes a sound like this: Moo! Moo!

FLANNEL BOARD ACTIVITY

Fiddle-I-Fee

(See pages 126-131 for song and patterns)

CRAFT

Patchwork Scarecrow

Glue the scarecrows onto craft sticks. Give the toddlers small pieces of scrap material or colored paper to glue onto the scarecrow. The dangling arms and legs are made with thick yarn and the construction paper hands and feet are taped or glued on. The arms and legs can be tied on ahead of time or you can ask the parents to do this.

Supplies Needed:

Heavy paper (for scarecrow's body)
Craft sticks
Pieces of scrap material or paper
Yarn
Construction paper
Glue sticks

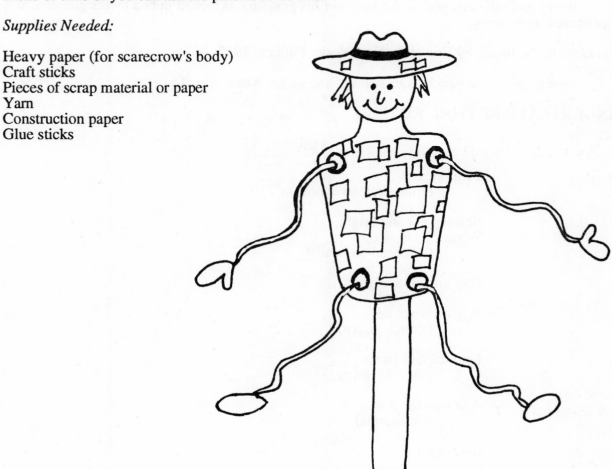

MORE BOOKS OF INTEREST

Adams, Pam	*Old MacDonald Had A Farm*
Hellard, Susan	*Time to Get Up*
Hill, Eric	*Spot Goes to the Farm*
Most, Bernard	*The Cow That Went Oink!*
Nakatani, Chiyoko	*My Day on the Farm*
Pizer, Abigail	*It's a Perfect Day*
Rockwell, Anne	*Willy Can Count*
Tafuri, Nancy	*Early Morning in the Barn*

FUN IN THE SUN

BOOKS

Where Does the Sun Go at Night? by Mirra Ginsburg, illus. Jose Aruego. New York: Greenwillow Books, 1981.

Every night the sun goes to the house of his grandma, is tucked in bed by his grandpa, and is awakened by morning.

Spot Goes to the Beach by Eric Hill. New York: Putnam, 1985.

Spot plays on the beach, goes fishing, and makes a new friend.

FINGERPLAYS/ACTION RHYMES

Sun

I am the sun
    (arms circle over head)

Shining hot and bright,
When I go to sleep
    (rest head on hands)

Day turns into night.

When I wake up,
    (stretch, yawn)

I stretch and yawn.
    (stretch, yawn)

And turn the darkness,
    (circle arms)

Into dawn.

Summer

A little girl went walking,
    (walk fingers on arm)

One lovely summer day
She saw a little rabbit,
That quickly hopped away.
    (hold up two fingers, hop them behind back)

She saw the shining river,
Go winding in and out
    (make wavy motions with head)

And little fishes in it,
Were playing all about.
      (put palms together making waving motion)

MUSIC

Mr. Sun

(For melody see Music Appendix, Song 11)

Oh Mister Sun, Sun, Mister Golden Sun,
Please shine down on me. Oh Mister Sun,
Sun, Mister Golden Sun, hiding behind a tree.

These little children are asking you
To please come out so we can play with you.
Oh Mister Sun, Sun, Mister Golden Sun, please
Shine down on me.

FLANNEL BOARD ACTIVITY

The Seashore

(See pages 111-113 for poem and patterns)

GAME

Roll a beach ball to each toddler and have them roll it back to you. You may want to use the ball bouncing rhyme on page 13.

CRAFT

Sun Visor

Cut toddler-sized visors out of poster board. Punch holes in both sides of the visor. Cut a large rubber band and tie both ends to the holes. If the visor is too tight add another cut rubber band. Let the toddlers decorate their visors with pom-poms, stickers, or glitter (closely supervise them when they use the glitter).

Supplies Needed:

Poster board
Rubber bands
Pom-Poms
Stickers
Glitter
Glue Sticks

(see illustration next page)

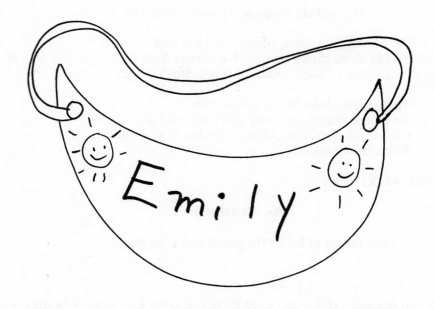

MORE BOOKS OF INTEREST

Dickens, Lucy — *Rosy's Pool*
Garland, Sarah — *Having A Picnic*
Hoban, Julia — *Amy Loves the Sun*
Rockwell, Anne — *At the Beach*
Rockwell, Harlow — *My Back Yard*
Seymour, Peter — *What's at the Beach?*
Sis, Peter — *Beach Ball*

WATER CREATURES

BOOKS

Busy Beavers by Lydia Dabcovich. New York: Dutton, 1988.

A day in the life of a beaver family as they swim, play, and build a dam.

Little Duck's Bicycle Ride by Dorothy Stott. New York: Dutton, 1991.

Follow little duck uphill and downhill, through the barnyard, over a bridge and splash!

FINGERPLAYS/ACTION RHYMES

Funny Duck

Waddle, waddle, waddle duck,
Waddle to the pond.
Paddle, paddle, paddle duck,
Paddle round and round
      (paddle with hands).

Tail up, head down, funny little duck,
Tail up, head down, funny little duck.
      (move head downward. Place hands
      behind back to represent tail)

The Little Frog

I am a little frog,
Hopping on a log,
      (hop fingers on palm of other hand)

Listen to my song.
      (make frog sounds)

I sleep all winter long,
      (place head on hands)

I wake up and peek out,
Up I jump, all about.
      (hop fingers on palm)

I catch flies,
      (grabbing motion)

I wink my eyes,
      (wink eyes)

I hop and hop,
      (stand and hop)

And then I stop.

PUPPETS

Perform the story *The Wide Mouthed Frog* by Rex Schneider, with hand puppets.

A wide mouthed frog asks several animals what type of food they like to eat. Then he meets an alligator whose favorite food is wide mouthed frogs.

You need not use all the characters in the picture book. A condensed cast of characters is listed below.

Puppets

Frog
Turtle
Raccoon
Squirrel
Alligator

MUSIC

Glack Goon

(For melody see Music Appendix, Song 12)

Glack Goon went the little green frog one day!
Glack Goon went the little green frog one day!
Glack Goon went the little green frog one day!
And his eyes went glack, glack, goon!

FLANNEL BOARD ACTIVITY

Five Little Ducks

(See pages 114-115 for song and patterns)

CRAFT

"Waddles" the Duck

Cut duck silhouettes out of white or yellow poster board or heavy paper. Cut two finger holes at the bottom. Let the toddlers glue on a beak and feathers.

Supplies Needed:

Poster board or heavy paper (white or yellow)
Orange construction paper (for beaks)
Feathers
Glue sticks

"Waddles" the Duck

MORE BOOKS OF INTEREST

Asch, Frank	*Turtle Tale*
Casey, Patricia	*Quack, Quack*
Ginsburg, Mirra	*The Chick and the Duckling*
Hayes, Sarah	*Nine Ducks, Nine*
Hellard, Susan	*The Ugly Duckling*
Paris, Pat	*The Frog*
Raffi	*Five Little Ducks*
Whybrow, Jan	*Quacky, quack-quack!*

KITTENS AND PUPPIES

BOOKS

Where's Spot? by Eric Hill. New York: Putnam, 1980.

Spot's mom, Sally, searches everywhere for him. She finds a striped snake in a clock, a lion under the stairs, a hippo in the piano, and, finally, Spot.

Who Said Meow? by Maria Polushkin. New York: Bradbury Press, 1988.

Who is making that sound? Puppy tries to find out which animal is making all that noise.

FINGERPLAYS/ACTION RHYMES

Two Puppy Dogs and a Kitten

Two little puppy dogs
    (hold up two fingers)

Lying fast asleep,
    (place head on hands)

Soft and wooly
All in a heap,
Along came a little kitten
    (tip-toe)

Creeping near, "Meow,"
She cried right in their ear.
    (cover ears)

Two little puppy dogs
    (hold up two fingers)

After one cat,
    (hold up one finger)

Did you ever play tag like that?

Where Has My Little Dog Gone?

Oh where, oh where has my little dog gone?
    (shade eyes, look around)

Oh where, oh where can he be?
With his ears cut short (touch ears)

And his tail cut long
    (wag hand behind back)

Oh where, oh where can he be?

- Nursery Song

MUSIC

Rags

(A dog puppet may be used to perform the action in this song)

(For melody and additional verse see Music Appendix, Song 14)

I've got a dog, his name is Rags,
He eats so much that his tummy sags,
His ears flip, flop and his tail wig, wags,
And when he walks, he walks zig, zag.
He goes flip, flop, wig, wag, zig, zag,
I love Rags and he loves me.
(repeat lines five and six twice)

FLANNEL BOARD ACTIVITY

Five Kittens in the Bed

(See pages 116-118 for poem and patterns)

CRAFT

Paper Cup Dog Puppet

Prepare the cups ahead of time by fastening them together with brads. Let the toddlers glue on the ears, legs, tail, and nose.

Supplies Needed:

Paper cups
Construction paper
Pom-poms (for nose)
Washable markers
Glue sticks

MORE BOOKS OF INTEREST

Allen, Pamela — *My Cat Maisie*

Astley, Judy — *When One Cat Woke Up*

Bridwell, Norman — *Where is Clifford*

Bryant, Donna — *My Dog Jessie*

Campbell, Rod — *Misty's Mischief*

Hersom, Kathleen and Donald — *The Copycat*

Keats, Ezra Jack — *Whistle For Willie*

Leman, Martin — *Ten Cats and Their Tales*

Zion, Gene — *Harry, the Dirty Dog*

JUNGLE SAFARI

BOOKS

A Rhinoceros Wakes Me Up in the Morning by Peter Goodspeed, illus. Dennis Panek.
New York: Bradbury Press, 1982.

Jungle animals help a little boy through his daily activities.

Crocodile Beat by Gail Jorgensen, illus. Patricia Mullins. New York: Bradbury Press, 1989.

A book full of noisy jungle animals and a sneaky crocodile.

FINGERPLAYS/ACTION RHYMES

Three Little Monkeys

Three little monkeys
    (hold up three fingers)

Swinging in a tree
    (move fingers back and forth)

Teasing Mr. Crocodile, "You can't catch me!"
    (wag one finger)

Along comes crocodile quiet as can be
    (palms together, make weaving motion)

And SNAP!
    (snap palms together)

Two little monkeys...(repeat above)

One little monkey...(repeat above and change last line)

SNAP! Ha, ha, you missed me!

The Spotted Giraffe

The spotted giraffe is tall as can be,
    (raise one arm high)

His lunch is a bunch of leaves off a tree.
    (make nibbling motion with fingers)

He has a very long neck and his legs are long too,
    (point to raised arm and legs)

And he can run faster than his friends at the zoo.

PUPPETS

Act out the story of *The Little Gorilla* by Ruth Bornstein with hand or stick puppets. Below is a list of characters that appear in the story. It's not necessary to use all the characters listed. You may want to adapt the story depending on the puppets you have available.

Puppets and Props

Little gorilla
Mother gorilla
Father gorilla
Grandma gorilla
Grandpa gorilla
Pink butterfly
Green parrot
Red monkey
Boa constrictor
Giraffe
Elephant
Lion
Hippo
Birthday cake (poster board cut-out)

MUSIC

Monkey See, Monkey Do

(For melody see Music Appendix, Song 15)

When you clap, clap, clap your hands,
The monkey clap, clap, claps his hands.
Monkey see and monkey do,
Monkey does the same as you.

When you stamp, stamp, stamp your feet,
The monkey stamp, stamp, stamps his feet.
Monkey see and monkey do,
Monkey does the same as you.

When you turn, turn, turn around,
The monkey turn, turn, turns around.
Monkey see and monkey do,
Monkey does the same as you.

When you jump, jump, jump up high,
The monkey jump, jump, jumps up high.
Monkey see and monkey do,
Monkey does the same as you.

FLANNEL BOARD ACTIVITY

The Lion and the Mouse

(For story and patterns see pages 119-120)

CRAFT

The Roaring Lion

Make a roaring lion mask by cutting eye holes and a mouth hole out of a paper plate. Let the children glue on a yarn mane and whiskers and construction paper nose and ears. Ask the parents to secure the cardboard tube to the back of the plate with masking tape.

Supplies Needed:

Cardboard tubes
Masking tape
Yarn cut in short lengths
Construction paper
Crayons
Glue sticks

MORE BOOKS OF INTEREST

Aruego, Jose   *We Hide, You Seek*
Ehlert, Lois   *Color Zoo*
Hawkins, Colin   *The Elephant*
Kasza, Kieko   *When Elephant Walks*
Morozumi, Atsuko   *One Gorilla*
Seymour, Peter   *What's in the Jungle*
Yoshida, Toshi   *Young Lions*
Ziefert, Harriet   *Going on a Lion Hunt*

THIS LITTLE PIGGY

BOOKS

This Little Piggy by Susan Hellard. New York: Putnam, 1989.

A lift-a-flap book which includes the little-known second verse of the rhyme, which is quite funny.

Piggies by Audrey Wood. San Diego: Harcourt Brace Jovanovich, 1991.

A beautifully illustrated large-format book which shows the antics of tiny piggies.

FINGERPLAYS/ACTION RHYMES

The Pigs

Piggie Wig and Piggie Wee,
    (hold up thumbs)

Hungry pigs as pigs could be,
For their dinner had to wait
Down behind the barnyard gate.
    (with palms facing body and fingertips
    touching, bring thumbs behind "gate")

Piggie Wig and Piggie Wee,
Greedy pigs as pigs could be, (wiggle thumbs)
For their dinner ran pellmell;
    (make scampering motion with hands)

In the trough both pigs fell.
    (cup hands to represent trough. Plop
    thumbs into palms)
                       - Emilie Poulsson

This Little Piggy

This little piggy went to market,
This little piggy stayed home.
This little piggy had roast beef,
This little piggy had none,
And this little piggy went
"Wee, Wee, Wee," all the way home.
                       - Old American Rhyme

PUPPETS

Perform the story of *The Three Little Pigs* using hand or stick puppets. Make cardboard silhouettes of the three houses and cut a window in each so that the pigs can be seen inside. Flip the straw and twig houses down flat when the wolf puppet blows them in. Have the first and second little pigs run away to the brick house.

MUSIC

The Oink Song

(For melody see Music Appendix, Song 16)

There was an old woman,
And she had a little pig.
Oink, oink, oink!
There was an old woman,
And she had a little pig.
It didn't eat much,
'Cause it wasn't very big.
Oink, oink, oink!

FLANNEL BOARD ACTIVITY

Five Little Pigs

(See pages 121-125 for poem and patterns)

CRAFT

Little Piggy Paper Plate Mask

Cut eye holes in paper plates. Glue or tape craft sticks to the plates. Give the toddlers noses and ears to glue on and crayons to draw the mouth with.

Supplies Needed:

Paper plates (pink if possible)
Craft sticks
Construction paper
Crayons
Glue sticks

(see illustration next page)

MORE BOOKS OF INTEREST

Galdone, Paul   *The Three Little Pigs*
Hawkins, Colin   *This Little Pig*
Hofstrand, Mary   *Albion Pig*
Peppi, Rodney   *Huxley Pig, The Clown*
Stepto, Michele   *Snuggle Piggy and the*
             Magic Blanket
Wheeler, Cindy   *Rose*

MARVELOUS MICE

BOOKS

Watch Where You Go by Sally Noll. New York: Greenwillow Books, 1990.

A little gray mouse makes a journey through a forest.

The Little Mouse, The Ripe Red Strawberry and the Big Hungry Bear by Don and Audrey Wood, illus. Don Wood. New York: Child's Play, 1984.

Little Mouse tries to hide a strawberry from the big hungry bear and finally figures out a perfect solution.

FINGERPLAYS/ACTION RHYMES

Mouse in a Hole

A mouse lived in a little hole,
    (hold up fist with thumb tucked inside)

Lived softly in a little hole.
When all was quiet as quiet can be...
Out popped he!
    (pop thumb out of fist)

Baby Mice

Where are the baby mice?
Squeak, squeak, squeak?
    (hold up fist)

I cannot see them.
Peek, peek, peek!
    (peek into fist)

Here they come out of their home in the wall.
One, two, three, four, five and this is all!
    (show one finger at a time)

PUPPETS

I'm a Little Mouse by Noelle Carter is a story of a little mouse searching for his mother. Using hand or stick puppets, perform the story with all or some of the characters listed below.

Puppets

Baby Mouse
Mother Mouse
Bear
Fish
Snake
Turtle

MUSIC

Hickory Dickory Dock

(For melody see Music Appendix, Song 17)

Hickory, dickory, dock,
The mouse ran up the clock.
The clock struck one,
The mouse ran down.
Hickory, dickory, dock.

FLANNEL BOARD ACTIVITY

The Lion and the Mouse

(For story and patterns see pages 119-120)

CRAFT

Peek-A-Boo Mouse Puppet

Glue or tape the mouse picture to the end of a drinking straw. Poke a hole in the bottom of a paper cup and slide the other end of the straw through the hole. This puppet may be used with the rhyme "Mouse in a Hole" on page 47. Be sure to make enough puppets ahead of time for all the children. Distribute them at the end of the program.

Supplies Needed:

Paper cups
Straws
Mouse picture
Glue or tape

Peek-A-Boo Mouse Puppet

Mouse puppet

BOOKS OF INTEREST

Carle, Eric	*Do You Want to be My Friend?*
Geraghty, Paul	*Look Out, Patrick!*
Ivimey, John	*Three Blind Mice*
Kraus, Robert	*Whose Mouse are You?*
Numeroff, Laura Joffe	*If You Give a Mouse a Cookie*
Stevens, Harry	*Fat Mouse*
Walsh, Ellen	*You Silly Goose*

49

COME TO THE ANIMAL FAIR

BOOKS

The Sheep Follow by Monica Wellington. New York: Dutton, 1992.

A herd of playful sheep follow various other animals until they are too tired to follow their shepherd.

I Went Walking by Sue Williams, illus. by Julie Vivas. San Diego: Harcourt Brace Jovanovich, 1989.

A little boy is followed by a menagerie of colorful animals.

FINGERPLAYS/ACTION RHYMES

The Elephant

The elephant looks like a giant,
    (stretch arms wide)

He is wrinkled and he is strong.
He has two big floppy ears,
    (make big ears with hands)

And a nose that's oh, so long!
    (clasp hands, swing arms)

He sways back and forth
Through the jungle he goes,
With his big floppy ears,
    (make big ears with hands)

And his hose of a nose.
    (clasp hands, swing arms)

Six Little Ducks

Six little ducks that I once knew,
Fat ones, skinny ones, pretty ones too.
    (arms wide for fat, close for skinny, flap hands for pretty)

But the one little duck with the feather on his back
    (turn to show back and wiggle fingers on back)

He led the others with his quack, quack, quack!
Quack, quack, quack!
Quack, quack, quack!
He led the others with his quack, quack, quack!
    (open and close one hand while quacking)

PUPPETS

Read *Roar and More* by Karla Kuskin as an assistant behind a table or puppet theater works the puppets and makes the animal sounds. The number of puppets you use for this story may be adapted.

Puppets

Lion
Elephant
Tiger
Snake
Kangaroo
Fish
Cat
Dog
Bee
Mouse
Giraffe

MUSIC

The Animal Fair

(For melody see Music Appendix, Song 18)

I went to the animal fair,
The birds and the beasts were there.
The big baboon by the light of the moon,
Was combing his orange hair.
The monkey bumped the skunk,
And climbed up the elephant's trunk.
The elephant sneezed and fell to his knees,
And that was the end of the monk,
The monk, the monk, the monk, the monk.

FLANNEL BOARD ACTIVITY

Fiddle-I-Fee

(See pages 126-131 for song and patterns)

CRAFT

Paper Bag Puppets

Allow the toddlers to color pre-cut pieces and glue them onto paper bags with the help of a parent.

MORE BOOKS OF INTEREST

Arnosky, Jim	*Watching Foxes*
Barrett, Judi	*Animals Should Definitely Not Wear Clothing*
Boynton, Sandra	*Moo Baa La La La*
deRegniers, Beatrice	*It Does Not Say Meow*
Guarino, Deborah	*Is Your Mama a Llama?*
Jensen, Kiersten	*Possum in the House*
Martin, Bill	*Polar Bear, Polar Bear, What Do You Hear?*
Williams, Garth	*Baby Animals*
Wood, Audrey	*Quick as a Cricket*

HERE A CHICK, THERE A CHICK

BOOKS

Good Morning, Chick by Mirra Ginsburg, illus. Byron Barton. New York: Mulberry, 1980.

The baby chick comes out of its house and goes out to explore the world.

Hatch, Egg, Hatch! by Shen Roddie. Boston: Little, Brown, 1991.

Mother Hen does everything possible to hatch her egg. Will she ever see her chick?

FINGERPLAYS/ACTION RHYMES

The Chicks

"Come little children,"
    (gesture to come over)

Calls Mother Hen.
"It's time to take
Your nap again."
And under the feathers,
The small chicks creep.
    (fingers creep under other hand)

And she clucks a song,
Till they fall asleep.
    (rest head on hands and close eyes)

Three Little Chicks

Three eggs sat on by Mother Hen,
    (hold up three fingers)

To keep them warm and then,
    (put fingers into cup of other hand)

Crack, crack, crack,
    (peek into hand)

Peep, peep, peep,
Three baby chicks softly cheep.
    (raise fingers and cheep)

MUSIC

I Had A Little Rooster

(For melody and additional verses see Music Appendix, Song 19)

I had a little rooster by the barnyard gate,
And that little rooster was my playmate.
And that little rooster sang: Cock-a-doodle-doo.
A-doodley, doodley, doodley-do.

FLANNEL BOARD ACTIVITY

The Little Red Hen

(For story and patterns see pages 132-135)

CRAFT

The Hatching Chick

Cut the egg pieces out of heavy paper and attach the two pieces with a brad. Let the toddlers glue pre-cut chicks onto the eggs. Give them small feathers and construction paper beaks to glue onto the chicks.

Supplies Needed:

Heavy white paper
Brads
Yellow construction paper (for chicks)
Orange construction paper (for beaks)
Feathers
Glue sticks
Washable markers

MORE BOOKS OF INTEREST

Brandenberg, Franz — *Cock-A-Doodle-Doo*
D'Aulaire, Ingri — *Don't Count Your Chicks*
Galdone, Paul — *Little Tuppen*
Hutchins, Pat — *Rosie's Walk*
Lillie, Patricia — *When the Rooster Crowed*
McMillan, Bruce — *Here a Chick, There a Chick*
Ormerod, Jan — *The Story of Chicken Licken*
Williams, Garth — *The Chicken Book*

YUMMY!

BOOKS

Fat, Fat Calico Cat by Donald Charles. Chicago: Childrens Press, 1977.

> Calico Cat likes to eat all kinds of sweets. But he ends up with a tummy ache.

What a Good Lunch by Shigeo Watanabe. New York: Philomel, 1991.

> Bear tries to find the best way to eat spaghetti, soup, and salad.

FINGERPLAYS/ACTION RHYMES

Jelly

Jelly on my head,
> (touch head)

Jelly on my toes,
> (touch toes)

Jelly on my shirt,
> (touch shirt)

Jelly on my nose.
> (touch nose)

Laughing and a-licking,
Having me a time,
> (waggle head)

Jelly on my belly,
> (rub belly)

But I like it fine.

Jelly is my favorite food,
And when I'm in a jelly mood,
> (pretend to eat jelly)

I can't ever get enough,
Of that yummy, gummy stuff.
> (rub belly)

A Cup of Tea

Here's a cup, and here's a cup
    (cup both hands to represent cups)

And here's a pot of tea.
    (bring both hands together in the shape of a pot)

Pour a cup, and pour a cup,
    (making pouring motion)

And have a drink with me.
    (pretend to drink from cup)

PUPPETS

Read or tell a simple version of *The Gingerbread Boy* as an assistant behind a puppet theater or table illustrates the action in the story with stick puppets.

Puppets

Old woman
Old man
Gingerbread boy
Cow
Pig
Bear
Fox

MUSIC

Peanut Butter and Jelly

(For melody and extra verses see Music Appendix, Song 20)

Peanut, peanut butter and jelly!
Peanut, peanut butter and jelly!
First you take the peanuts and you crush'em,
You crush'em, you crush'em, crush'em
crush'em, singing
Peanut, peanut butter and jelly!

FLANNEL BOARD ACTIVITY

Five Little Cookies

(See pages 136-137 for poem and patterns)

CRAFT/SNACK

Decorate Your Own Cupcake

Provide the toddlers with cupcakes to frost and decorate. Distribute several small bowls of frosting and a variety of cake decorations. Tongue depressors or craft sticks may be used to spread frosting.

MORE BOOKS OF INTEREST

Carle, Eric — *The Very Hungry Caterpillar*
Degen, Bruce — *Jamberry*
Demarest, Chris — *No Peas for Nellie*
Garland, Sarah — *Having a Picnic*
Gomi, Taro — *Who Ate It?*
Numeroff, Laura — *If You Give a Mouse a Cookie*
Westcott, Nadine — *Peanut Butter and Jelly*
Wheeler, Cindy — *Marmalade's Picnic*

DADDY AND ME

BOOKS

A Perfect Father's Day by Eve Bunting. New York: Clarion, 1991.

Susie treats her father to a series of special activities for Father's Day.

Papa, Please Get the Moon For Me by Eric Carle. Natick, MA: Picture Book Studio, 1991.

Monica's father gets the moon out of the sky for her. The book has several large fold-out pages.

FINGERPLAYS/ACTION RHYMES

See Me Grow

When I was a baby,
I was very, very small.
       (squat down make self small)

Then I grew and grew,
And grew and grew.
       (slowly stretch up)

Look at me, Daddy!
I'm TALL!

Dance to Your Daddy

Dance to your Daddy,
My little boy.
Dance to your Daddy,
My little girl.
You shall get a fishy,
In a little dishy.
You shall get a fishy,
When the boat comes in.

- Nursery Rhyme

MUSIC

I Love Daddy

(Sung to: "Frere Jacques")

I love Daddy, I love Daddy,
Yes I do, Yes I do.
We have fun together,
We have fun together,
Just us two, just us two.

- Diane Briggs

FLANNEL BOARD ACTIVITY

Where's My Daddy

(For story and patterns see pages 138-143)

CRAFT

A Picture of Me

Using pieces of white paper wide and long enough for the toddlers to lie down on, have the fathers quickly trace the outline of their child's body. Next they can work with their child as they draw and color the face, hair, and clothes.

Supplies Needed:

White paper (large)
Washable markers or crayons

MORE BOOKS OF INTEREST

Asch, Frank	*Just Like Daddy*
Bunting, Eve	*No Nap*
Das, Carla	*Are You My Daddy?*
McPhail, David	*Emma's Pet*
Ormerod, Jan	*Dad's Back*
Porter-Gaylord, Laurel	*I Love My Daddy Because*
Stewart, Robert	*The Daddy Book*
Watanabe, Shigeo	*Daddy, Play With Me!*

WHAT WILL I WEAR?

BOOKS

A Fox Got My Socks by Hilda Offen. New York: Dutton, 1992.

    The wind blows a toddler's laundry away and a menagerie of animals ends up wearing it.

How Do I Put It On? by Shigeo Watanabe, illus. Yasuo Ohtomo. New York: Philomel, 1977.

    After much trial and error, little bear, finally, gets dressed all by himself.

FINGERPLAYS/ACTION RHYMES

Shoes

Baby's shoes,
Mother's shoes,
Father's shoes,
Policeman's shoes,
GIANT SHOES!

(Put hands close together to show the size of baby shoes and move hands farther apart for each size. Stretch arms wide for giant shoes.)

This is the Way

(Tune: "Here We Go 'Round the Mulberry Bush")

This is the way we put on our shirt,
Put on our shirt, put on our shirt.
This is the way we put on our shirt,
So early in the morning.

This is the way we put on our pants...
This is the way we put on our shoes...
This is the way we put on our hat...

PUPPETS

    Use a girl puppet to play the part of Jenny, as you read or tell the story of *Jenny's Hat* by Ezra Jack Keats. Put a hat on the puppet and place the appropriate objects on the hat according to the story. Be sure to adapt and simplify this story for toddlers.

Puppets and Props

Girl puppet with hat
Bird puppet
Flowers
Colored eggs
Paper fan
Pictures
Red rose
Yellow rose
Pink valentine
Bird's nest

MUSIC

Mary Wore a Red Dress

(For melody see Music Appendix, Song 21)

Mary wore a red dress, red dress, red dress,
Mary wore a red dress all day long.
Ethan wore his purple pants, purple pants, purple pants
Ethan wore his purple pants all day long.
Molly wore her yellow hat, yellow hat, yellow hat,
Molly wore her yellow hat all day long.

*(Choose children from your audience and sing
about what they're wearing)*

FLANNEL BOARD ACTIVITY

Getting Dressed

(See pages 144-145 for poem and patterns)

ACTIVITY

Provide dress-up clothes for the toddlers to try on. Be sure to include lots of shoes, hats, ties, and costume jewelry. Mirrors are a must also.

CRAFT

Dinosaur Dress Up

Provide the toddlers with pictures of dinosaurs and pre-cut clothing, hats, and shoes to paste onto them.

Supplies Needed:

Photocopies of animals
Pre-cut clothing
Glue sticks

MORE BOOKS OF INTEREST

Barrett, Judi   *Animals Should Definitely*
                                 Not Wear Clothing

Bruna, Dick   *I Can Dress Myself*
Carlstrom, Nancy   *Jesse Bear, What Will You Wear?*
Roffey, Maureen   *Look There's My Hat*
Slobodkina, Esphyr   *Caps for Sale*
Ziefert, Harriet   *Let's Get Dressed*

BUSY BUGS AND CATERPILLAR CAPERS

BOOKS

The Very Busy Spider by Eric Carle. New York: Philomel, 1984.

The spider spins a web that you can feel, making this book accessible to blind and sighted children.

In the Tall, Tall Grass by Denise Fleming. New York: Holt, 1991.

Follow a curious caterpillar as he makes a journey through the tall grass and sees many other insects including bees, ants, and fireflies.

FINGERPLAYS/ACTION RHYMES

Caterpillars

"Let's go to sleep," the little caterpillars said,
    (bend fingers into palms)

As they tucked themselves into their bed.
They will awaken by and by,
    (slowly unfold fingers)

And each one will be a lovely butterfly!
    (make flying motion with hands)

Eency Weency Spider

The eency-weency spider went up the water spout,
    (wiggle fingers upward)

Down came the rain and washed the spider out.
    (wiggle fingers for rain, sweep arms outward)

Out came the sun and dried up all the rain,
    (circle arms overhead)

And the eency-weency spider went up the spout again.
    (wiggle fingers upward)

PUPPETS

Tell the story of *The Very Hungry Caterpillar* by Eric Carle while you manipulate a caterpillar puppet through cardboard cut-outs of fruits and picnic foods (be sure to cut holes in the food). Reversible caterpillar/butterfly puppets are available through puppet manufacturers or you can design your own puppet with a tube sock. Sew wings to the inside of a caterpillar sock puppet. Reverse the sock at the end of the story.

MUSIC

Baby Bumble Bee

(For melody see Music Appendix, Song 22)

Oh, I'm bringing home a baby bumble bee,
Won't my mommy be so proud of me,
'Cause I'm bringing home a baby bumble bee.
Buzzy, buzzy, buzzy-OOH, he stung me!

FLANNEL BOARD ACTIVITY

Fuzzy, Wuzzy Caterpillar

(See pages 146-149 for poem and patterns)

CRAFT

Clothespin Butterfly

Let the toddlers decorate pieces of colored tissue paper with washable markers and glitter (when using glitter supervise closely). After they finish, ask the parents to help put the "wings" on the butterfly. Pipe cleaners may be used to make antennae.

Supplies Needed:

Tissue Paper
Washable markers
Glitter
Glue sticks
Clothespins
Pipe cleaners

(see illustration next page)

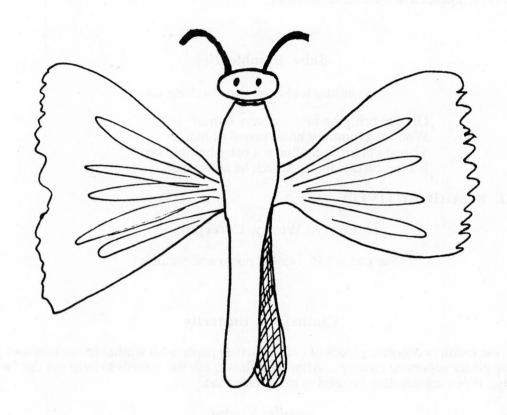

MORE BOOKS OF INTEREST

Barton, Byron   *Buzz! Buzz! Buzz!*
Carle, Eric   *The Grouchy Ladybug*
Carter, David   *How Many Bugs in a Box?*
Gomi, Taro   *Hi, Butterfly*
Kent, Jack   *The Caterpillar and the Polliwog*
Lionni, Leo   *Inch by Inch*
Pelham, David   *Worms Wiggle*
Wahl, Jan   *Follow Me Cried Bee*

TRICK OR TREAT

BOOKS

My First Halloween by Tomie de Paola. New York: Putnam, 1991.

Shows the fun of trick-or-treating, jack-o'-lanterns, and funny costumes.

Whooo's a Fright on Halloween Night? by Beau Gardner. New York: Putnam, 1990.

A pull-the-tab and spin-about book with black cats, spiders, jack-o'-lanterns, ghosts, and more.

FINGERPLAYS/ACTION RHYMES

A Very Old Witch

A very old witch was stirring a pot,
(make stirring motion)

O-o-o-o two little ghosts said,
What has she got?
Tippy-toe, tippy-toe, tippy-toe,
(tip-toe)

Booo!

Witch's Cat

I am the witch's cat,
Meow, meow, meow.
My fur is black as darkest night.
(stroke arm)

My eyes are glaring green and bright.
(point to eyes)

I am the witch's cat,
Meow, meow, meow.

PUPPETS

Read *The Halloween Pumpkin* by Pamela Oldfield. In this story, a big jack-o'-lantern on a stick goes about scaring people, until he meets up with a pig who is very hungry. While you read the story, have an assistant manipulate the puppets. The puppeteer should say the pumpkin's line: "OO-AH! OO-AH!"

Puppets

Old woman
Baker
Fisherman
Farmer
Pig
Pumpkin on a stick

MUSIC

I'm An Orange Pumpkin

(Tune: "I'm a Little Teapot")

I'm an orange pumpkin fat and round,
     (hold arms out to indicate roundness)
Sitting in the cornfield on the ground.
     (squat down)
Maybe I'll be a jack-o'-lantern,
With two big eyes.
     (circle eyes with fingers)
Or maybe I'll be made into,
A big fat pie.
     (make pie shape with arms)

FLANNEL BOARD ACTIVITY

Five Little Pumpkins

(See pages 150-151 for poem and patterns)

ACTIVITY

Be sure to give the toddlers a chance to show off their costumes. Lead them, with the help of their parents, on a parade through the library.

CRAFT

Pop-Up Ghost Giveaway

Place a cotton ball in the center of a tissue. Use a rubber band to form a neck. Insert a drinking straw into the neck. Put the other end of the straw through the bottom of a paper cup. Draw on the eyes and mouth. Lollipops may be used instead of cotton balls. But be sure all the parents are agreeable to this. Secure the lollipops to the drinking straws.

Supplies Needed:

Tissues
Rubber bands
Cotton balls or lollipops
Drinking straws
Paper cups
Markers

MORE BOOKS OF INTEREST

Asch, Frank   *Popcorn*
Balian, Lorna   *Humbug Witch*
Friskey, Margaret   *The Perky Little Pumpkin*
Gibbons, Gail   *Halloween*
Sendak, Maurice   *Where the Wild Things Are*
Stinson, Kathy   *The Dress Up Book*
Titherington, Jeanne   *Pumpkin, Pumpkin*
Ziefert, Harriet   *Who Can Boo the Loudest?*

TODDLER SNOW PARTY

BOOKS

The Snowy Day by Ezra Jack Keats. New York: Viking, 1962.

    Peter puts on his red snowsuit and goes outside to explore the snow-covered world.

The First Snowfall by Anne and Harlow Rockwell. New York: Macmillan, 1987.

    The beauty and fun of a first snowfall as seen by a little girl.

FINGERPLAYS/ACTION RHYMES

Roll Him Until He Is Big

Roll him and roll him until he is big,
    (make rolling motion)

Roll him until he is fat as a pig.
    (hold arms out to indicate roundness)

He has two eyes and a hat on his head,
    (fingers circle eyes, touch head with hands)

He'll stand there all night,
While we go to bed.
    (place head on hands, close eyes)

Winter

Here's a great big hill,
    (hold arms out to indicate hill)

With snow all down the side.
    (wiggle fingers downward)

Let's take our speedy sleds.
    (place hand on shoulder)

And down the hill we'll slide!
    (slide hand down arm)

PUPPETS

    Create a simple snowman puppet out of two layers of felt. Using heavy paper or poster board, make a pipe, a button nose, eyes, a black hat, and a broomstick. Glue pieces of Velcro to the back of each item. Sing "Frosty the Snowman" while adding the items to the puppet.

MUSIC

I'm a Little Snowman

(Tune: "I'm a Little Teapot")

I'm a little snowman short and fat,
    (sink down and indicate roundness with arms)
Here is my broomstick, and here is my hat.
    (hold up clasped hand and touch head)
When the sun comes out I melt away,
    (circle arms overhead)
Down, down, down, down I'm a puddle.
    (squat down and lower head)

FLANNEL BOARD ACTIVITY

Five Little Snowpeople

(See pages 152-154 for poem and patterns)

CRAFT

Build a Snowperson

Provide the toddlers with construction paper snowpeople pieces (a head, middle, and bottom). Distribute construction paper snowpeople accessories such as broomsticks, hats, carrot noses, and scarves. Let the toddlers glue the pieces onto a construction paper background.

Supplies Needed:

Construction paper
Glue sticks
Washable crayons or markers

MORE BOOKS OF INTEREST

Brett, Jan	*The Mitten*
Briggs, Raymond	*The Snowman Flap Book*
Burningham, John	*The Snow*
Dabcovich, Lydia	*Sleepy Bear*
Hoff, Syd	*When Will It Snow*
Komeda, Beverly	*The Winter Days*
Kuskin, Karla	*In the Flaky Frosty Morning*

ALL ABOUT ME

BOOKS

My Hands Can by Jean Holzenthaler, illus. by Nancy Tafuri. New York: Dutton, 1978.

Describes the various activities of a little person's hands.

I See by Rachel Isadora. New York: Greenwillow, 1985.

A little child responds to all of the things she sees.

FINGERPLAYS/ACTION RHYMES

Penny Thumbkin

(Tune: "Little Robin Redbreast")

Penny thumbkins upstairs,
    (move thumbs upward)

Penny thumbkins down,
    (move thumbs below shoulders)

Penny thumbkins dancing,
    (dance thumbs)

All around the town.
Dancing on my shoulders,
    (dance thumbs on shoulders)

Dancing on my head,
    (dance thumbs on head)

Dancing on my knees now,
    (dance thumbs on knees)

Tuck them into bed.
    (tuck thumbs under arms)

Repeat with:

Pointer finger...
Tall finger...
Ringer finger...
Pinky finger...
Family is...

Hands on Shoulders

Hands on shoulders, hands on knees,
Hands behind you, if you please.
Touch your hair,
Now your toes.
Hands up high in the air,
Down at your sides, now touch your hair.
Hands up high, as before.
Now clap your hands, one, two, three, four!

MUSIC

If You're Happy

(For melody see Music Appendix, Song 23)

If you're happy and you know it,
Clap your hands!
If you're happy and you know it,
Clap your hands!
If you're happy and you know it,
Then you really ought to show it.
If you're happy and you know it,
Clap your hands!

FLANNEL BOARD ACTIVITY

Getting Dressed

(See pages 144-145 for poem and patterns)

CRAFT

"Me"

Give each toddler a body silhouette approximately ten inches high. Give them washable markers or crayons, yarn for hair, and let them create.

Supplies Needed:

Heavy paper
Washable markers or crayons
Yarn
Glue sticks

(see illustration next page)

Body Silhouette

MORE BOOKS OF INTEREST

Bradman, Tony
Burningham, John
Galvani, Maureen
Garland, Sarah
Isadora, Rachel
Rockwell, Harlow
Roe, Eileen

This Little Baby
The Friend
What Can You Feel?
Going Shopping
I Touch
My Nursery School
All I Am

SLEEPYTIME STORIES

BOOKS

Asleep, Asleep by Mirra Ginsburg, illus. Nancy Tafuri. New York: Greenwillow Books, 1992.

>   All the animals and birds of the forest go to sleep, and then it is the little child's bedtime as well.

Where Does the Brown Bear Go? by Nicki Weiss. New York: Greenwillow Books, 1989.

>   A story that asks where different animals go when night comes and it's time to sleep.

FINGERPLAYS/ACTION RHYMES

Here is the Baby

Here is the baby ready for his nap,
>   (hold up one finger)

Lay him down in his mommy's lap.
>   (lay finger in palm of hand)

Cover him up, so he won't peep,
>   (close hand over finger)

Rock the baby fast asleep.
>   (rock hands back and forth)

Bedtime

Before I jump into my bed
>   (jump fingers into palm of other hand)

Before I dim the light
>   (turn out light)

I put my shoes together
>   (hands together)

So they can talk at night
>   (make talking motion with fingers)

I'm sure they would be lonesome
>   (make sad face)

If I tossed one here and there
>   (make tossing motion)

So I put them close together
>   (hands together)

For they're a friendly pair

Star Light, Star Bright

Star light, star bright,
First star I've seen tonight.
I wish I may, I wish I might,
Have the wish I wish tonight.
(make twinkling motion with hand)
- *Mother Goose*

PUPPETS

Use a talking-mouth girl puppet to act out the story *Lisa Can't Sleep* by Kaj Beckman. This is the story of a little girl who wants all her toys and stuffed animals in her bed before she goes to sleep.

Puppets and Props

Little girl puppet
Mother puppet
Bed
Lion
Lamb
Doll
Teddy bear
Dog
Cat
Rabbit
Jumping jack
Duck
Ball

MUSIC

Bluebird

(For melody and additional verse see Music Appendix, Song 24)

Bluebird, bluebird, through my window,
Bluebird, bluebird, through my window,
Bluebird, bluebird, through my window,
Oh, Mommy I'm so tired.

FLANNEL BOARD ACTIVITY

Hush Little Baby

(See pages 155-158 for song and patterns)

CRAFT

Twinkling Star

Glue construction paper stars onto craft sticks. Let the toddlers decorate the stars with crayons and glitter. Supervise them carefully as they add the glitter. Sing the song "Twinkle, Twinkle Little Star" to end the storytime.

Supplies Needed:

Construction paper
Craft sticks
Crayons
Glitter
Glue sticks

MORE BOOKS OF INTEREST

Aliki	*Hush Little Baby*
Baker, Alan	*Goodnight, William*
Beckman, Kaj	*Lisa Can't Sleep*
Brown, Margaret Wise	*Goodnight Moon*
Hutchins, Pat	*Goodnight Owl*
Ormerod, Jan	*Sleeping*
Pomerantz, Charlotte	*All Asleep*
Rice, Eve	*Goodnight, Goodnight*

PART II: FLANNEL BOARD ACTIVITIES FOR TODDLERS

THE FLANNEL BOARD

The flannel board is an essential ingredient in a successful toddler storytime. For toddlers the flannel board has a magical quality. They are fascinated when they see the storyteller place the figures on the board and take them off. Although flannel board story figures are two dimensional, as are the illustrations in books, they seem real to the toddler because they can be touched, handled, and moved. Therefore, flannel board activities hold the attention of toddlers very effectively.

Flannel boards can be made very easily from a rectangle of fiberboard, plywood, foamboard, or heavy cardboard. The patterns in this book will work well on a board approximately 34" wide by 24" high. Cover your board with flannel, felt, or Velcro compatible fabric. Many other fuzzy fabrics may also be used. Choose a color that will provide a good contrast to your story figures, allowing them to stand out. If the cloth on your board becomes soiled or worn, simply replace it with new cloth, perhaps in a different color.

HOW TO MAKE STORY FIGURES

Story figures may be made from felt, fabric, or paper. If you choose to make them with paper, use heavy paper, color or paint the figures attractively, and, if possible, laminate them. Be sure to attach a piece of Velcro or felt to the back.

Figures made with felt tend to be the most eye catching because of the texture of the fabric and the vibrant colors. Fabric stores stock a wide range of colors pre-cut into squares. Below is a list of tips for making attractive story figures with felt.

1. To make your felt figures stiff and easy to handle, make them with two layers of of felt and glue tracing paper or onion skin typing paper between the two layers. Use a strong fabric glue.

2. For eyes glue on beads, googly eyes, paper eyes, or use fabric paint.

3. Use a black felt-tip pen or fabric paint to draw lines to define an arm or a leg. Test your pen or paint on a scrap of felt first to get the desired effect.

4. Use yarn, sequins, beads, feathers, and other interesting materials to decorate your story figures.

MY LITTLE FISH

(by Diane Briggs)

I have a lovely fish tank,
Where my fish swim 'round and 'round.
And though their mouths are always moving,
They never make a sound.

This one's name is Whiskers,
He likes to clean the tank.
He dwells upon the bottom,
And eats everything that sank.

This one's name is Bubbles,
This one's name is Toby,
This one's name is Wanda,
And this one's name is Moby.

And here is a fish who is very special,
I named her Goldie Rose.
Once when I dropped my ring in the water,
She brought it up on her nose!

My darling little goldfish,
I do love them so.
With pretty shiny scales and tails,
Swimming to and fro.

Directions

Add the fish to the flannel board as you name them. Place the ring on the nose of the last fish when you say the last line of verse four.

MY LITTLE FISH

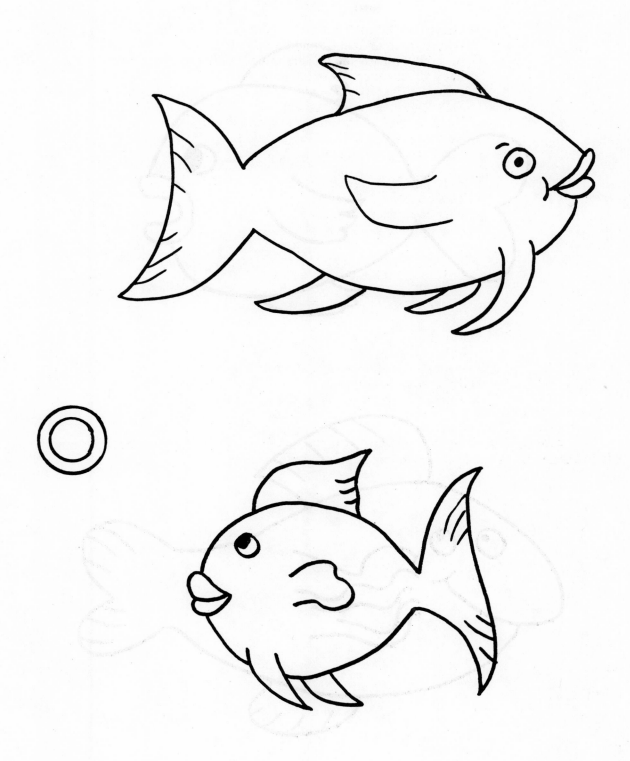

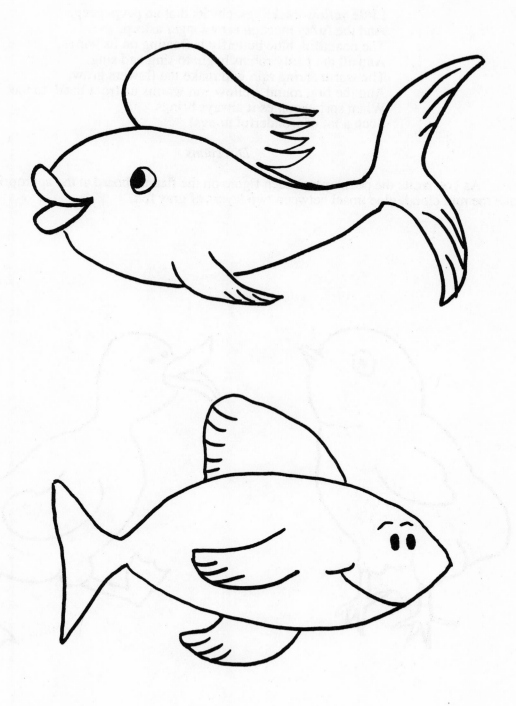

SOME THINGS THAT SPRING BRINGS

(by Diane Briggs)

Little yellow ducklings, chicks that go peep, peep,
And the fuzzy raccoon is no longer asleep.
The beautiful, blue butterfly is floating on its wings,
And all the pretty robins begin to sing and sing.
The warm spring rain will make the flowers grow,
And the big, round, yellow sun warms us from head to toe.
When spring comes it always brings,
Such a lot of wonderful things!

Directions

As you recite the poem, place each figure on the flannel board at the appropriate time. To make the rain cloud, glue tinsel between two layers of gray felt.

SOME THINGS THAT SPRING BRINGS

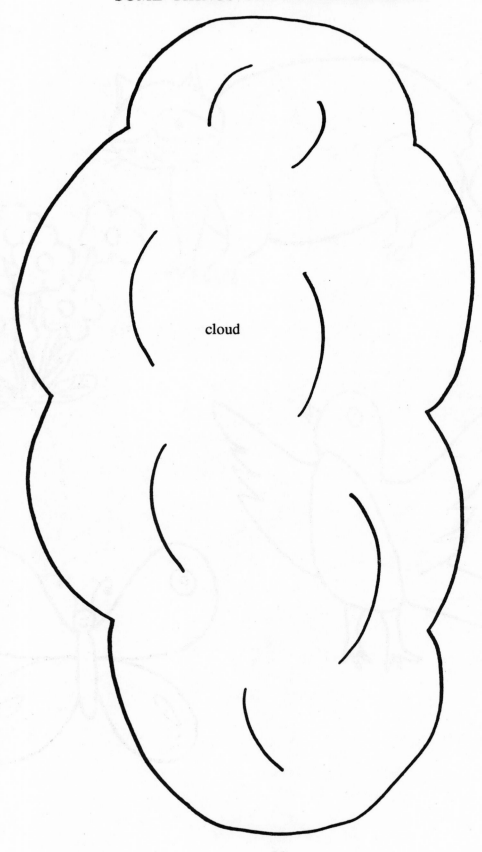

cloud

SOME THINGS THAT SPRING BRINGS

THE TORTOISE AND THE HARE

(A Fable from Aesop)

Once there was a tortoise and a hare. The hare could run very fast. But the tortoise was very slow. The hare would laugh at the tortoise and say, "You are the slowest creature I've ever seen. Do you ever get anywhere?"

One day the tortoise was tired of hearing the hare laugh at him and he said, "Let's have a race and I'll show you that I'm faster than you think." The hare agreed to the race.

They marked off a finish line and then the race began. The hare was soon far ahead of the tortoise. He was sure he could win so he decided to take a nap behind a nearby bush. The tortoise was still coming very slowly down the road.

After a while he passed the hare, who was still sleeping very peacefully.

The hare did not wake up until the tortoise was right at the finish line. The hare ran as fast as he could. But he couldn't catch up. The tortoise won the race!

Directions

Draw a face and other details on both sides of the hare so he can face either direction during the story.

When you begin to tell the story, place the hare and tortoise on the left side of the board and the bush in the middle. Put the finish-line marker on the right side of the board. When the hare takes a nap, put him behind the bush on his back.

MARVELOUS MUD

(by Diane Briggs)

Mud, mud, marvelous mud,
There was a boy who loved to jump in the mud.
He jumped and jumped and did not stop,
And then a little puppy jumped right in on top.

They rolled and they rolled, they were quite a sight,
Until the mommy came and cried: "Oh what a fright!"
She said, "Get in the tub right this minute!"
So the dog and the boy decided to quit it.

They got in the tub,
And they were soaped, scrubbed, and rubbed.
"Don't scrub so hard, Mom," the little boy said,
But she went right on scrubbing and then soaped up his head.

When the bath was over they were shiny and clean,
But a little while later they both could be seen,
Rolling around in the marvelous mud,
The boy and his puppy, how they did love mud.

Directions

Cut out an oval of brown felt to represent the mud. Glue face and clothing details on both sides of the boy and make the puppy figure reversible as well. Make one side look muddy by applying brown fabric paint or pieces of brown felt. When the boy and puppy get in the mud, flip them over to show their muddy side. After they take a bath flip them over again. Place the boy and the puppy behind the tub and "scrub" them with the brush.

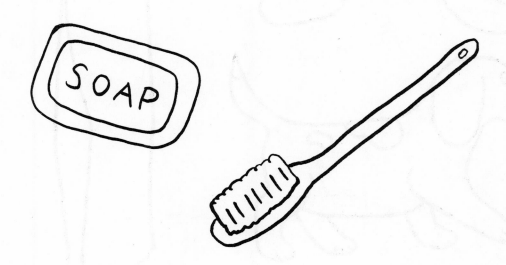

MARVELOUS MUD

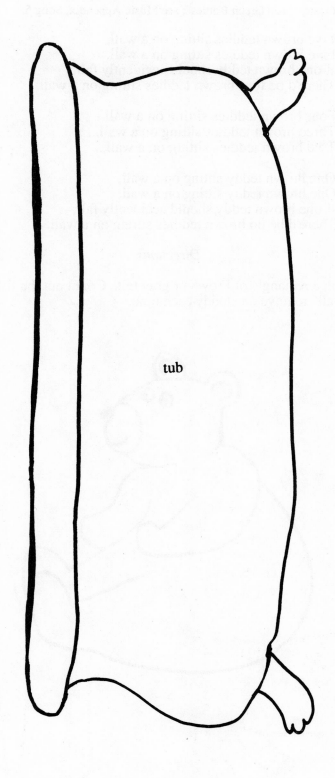

tub

FIVE BROWN TEDDIES

(Tune: "Ten Green Bottles"; see Music Appendix, Song 5)

Five brown teddies sitting on a wall,
Five brown teddies sitting on a wall,
If one brown teddy should accidently fall,
There'd be four brown teddies sitting on a wall.

Four brown teddies sitting on a wall...
Three brown teddies sitting on a wall...
Two brown teddies sitting on a wall...

One brown teddy sitting on a wall,
One brown teddy sitting on a wall,
If one brown teddy should accidently fall,
There'd be no brown teddies sitting on a wall.

Directions

Make a wall with a rectangle of brown or gray felt. Count out the five teddies as you place them on the wall. On "fall" remove one teddy each time.

FIVE BROWN TEDDIES

LOTS OF VALENTINES

(by Diane Briggs)

I've made a lot of valentines,
I'd like to give away,
Red ones, pink ones, blue ones,
On this February day.

Some of them have cupids,
Some of them have bows,
Some of them have tiny hearts,
And this one has a rose.

Come and get your valentines,
And tell me what you think.
Do you like the red or blue,
Or the ones I colored pink?

Directions

Make several paper valentines using the patterns and/or design some of your own. Be sure to make enough for all the children who attend the program.

As you say the poem place the valentines on the flannel board (a small piece of felt glued on the back of each one will ensure that they will stick). Let the toddlers come up and get a valentine after you say the poem.

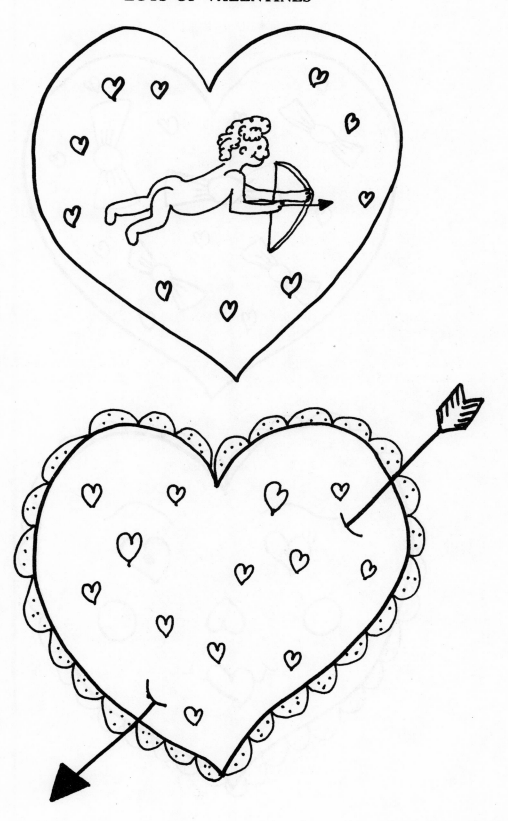

I SAW A GIRAFFE DRIVE BY*

(by Diane Briggs)

One sunny day I saw a giraffe drive by,
In a shiny car and a big bow tie.
Then I saw a sheep,
Riding in a jeep.
Then I saw a duck,
Driving a truck,
One sunny day.

One sunny day, I saw a platypus,
He was going for a ride on a little orange school bus.
Then I saw a goat,
She was rowing a boat.
Then I saw a bear,
Flying through the air,
One sunny day.

Oh, me, oh, my,
What a lot of funny animals went by!

* May be sung to the tune of "Down By the Bay"

Directions

Place the animals on the flannel board in succession as you recite or sing the poem.

101

I SAW A GIRAFFE DRIVE BY

THE NANNY

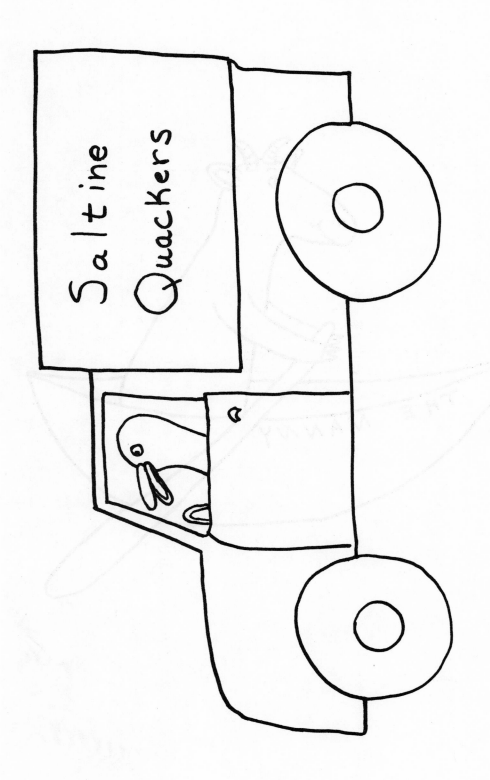

I SAW A GIRAFFE DRIVE BY

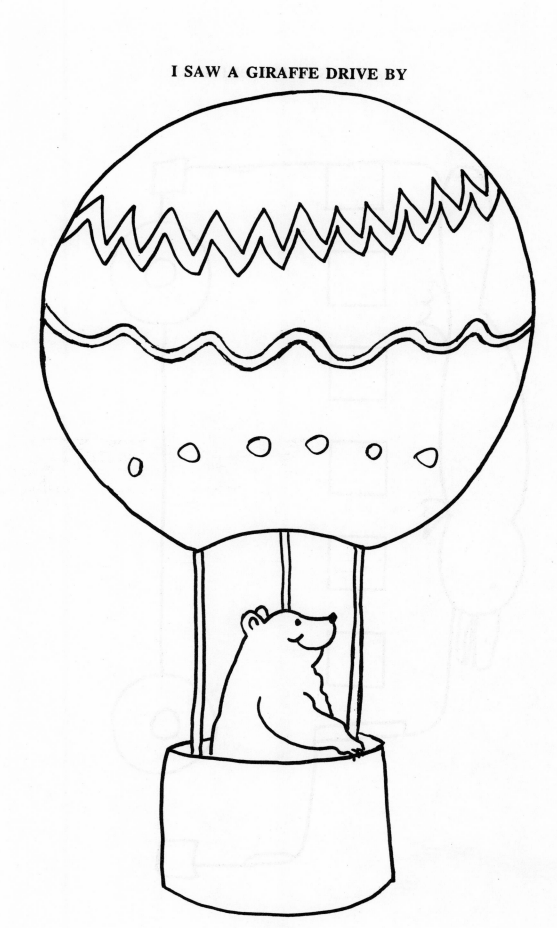

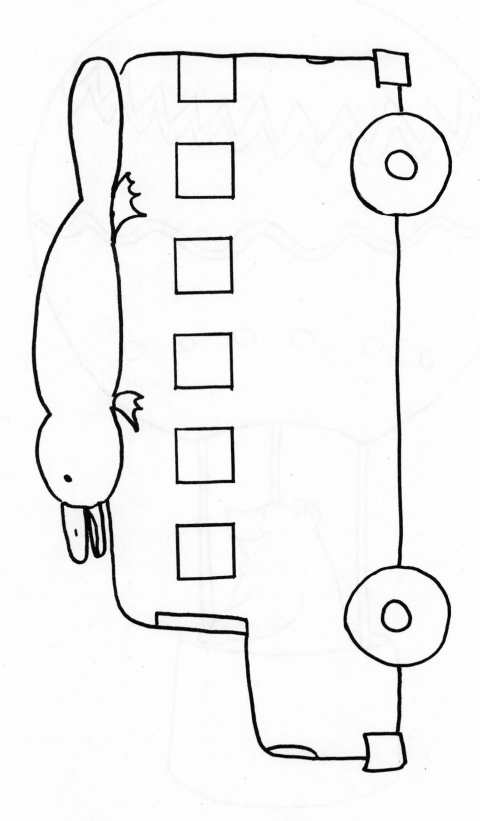

OLD MOTHER GOOSE

(Nursery Rhyme)

Old Mother Goose,
When she wanted to wander,
Would ride through the air,
On a very fine gander.

Mother Goose had a house,
'Twas built in a wood,
Where an owl at the door
For sentinel stood.

She had a son Jack,
A plain-looking lad,
He was not very good,
Yet not very bad.

She sent him to market,
A live goose he bought;
See, mother, says he,
I have not been for nought.

Jack's goose and her gander
Grew very fond;
They'd both eat together,
Or swim in the pond.

Jack found one fine morning,
As I have been told,
His goose had laid him
An egg of pure gold.

Jack ran to his mother.
The news for to tell,
She called him a good boy,
And said it was well.

Directions

Place the figures on the flannel board in succession as you recite the poem.

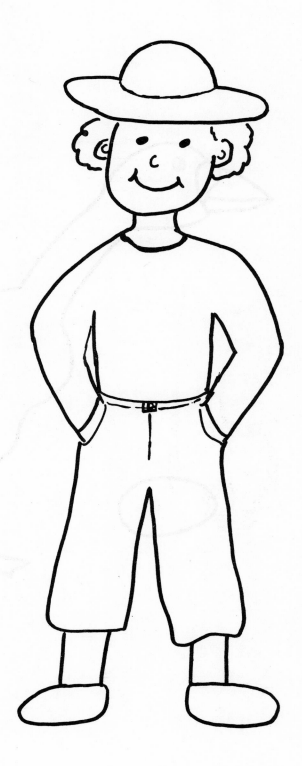

THE SEASHORE

(by Diane Briggs)

On a summer's day at the seashore,
I gather up lots of shells.
And build a castle in the sand,
And run up all the hills.

I brought my bucket and a shovel,
And I dug a hole so deep.
I found a crusty star fish,
I think that I will keep.

Directions

Add the objects to the flannel board in succession as you recite the poem.

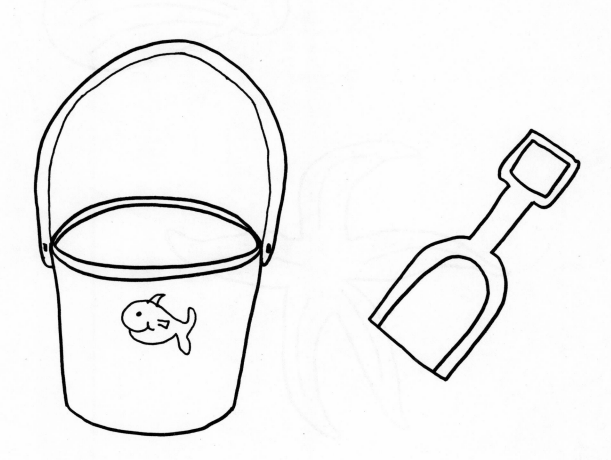

THE SEASHORE

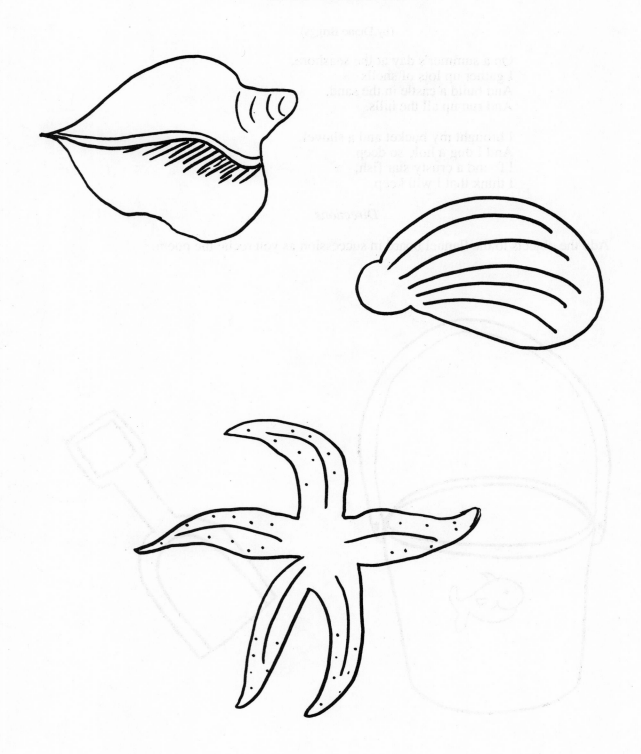

FIVE LITTLE DUCKS

(For melody see Music Appendix, Song 13)

Five little ducks went out one day,
Over the hills and far away.
Mother duck said, "Quack, quack, quack, quack!"
But only four little ducks came back.

Four little ducks...
Three little ducks...
Two little ducks...
One little duck...

Sad mother duck went out one day...
And all of the five little ducks came back!

Directions

Cut hill shapes out of green felt. Make five little ducks with the pattern. Before beginning the song, put the hills on the middle of the flannel board and the ducks on the right. On "Over the hills," move each little duck to the left of the hills. Bring one less duck back each time. At the end of the song bring all the ducks back to the right side of the flannel board. Encourage the toddlers to quack loudly on each refrain.

FIVE KITTENS IN THE BED

(Adapted from "Ten in the Bed")

There were five kittens in the bed,
And the little on said, "Rollover, I'm crowded."
So they all rolled over, and one fell out;

There were four kittens in the bed...
There were three kittens in the bed...
There were two kittens in the bed...

There was one kitten in the bed, and the
little one said, "I'm lonely."

So they all got back in the bed, and
the little one said, "Good Night!"

Directions

Put all the kittens on the bed. On "one fell out," remove one kitten from the bed each time until only the "little one" is left. Finally, put all the kittens back in the bed and cover them with the blanket.

116

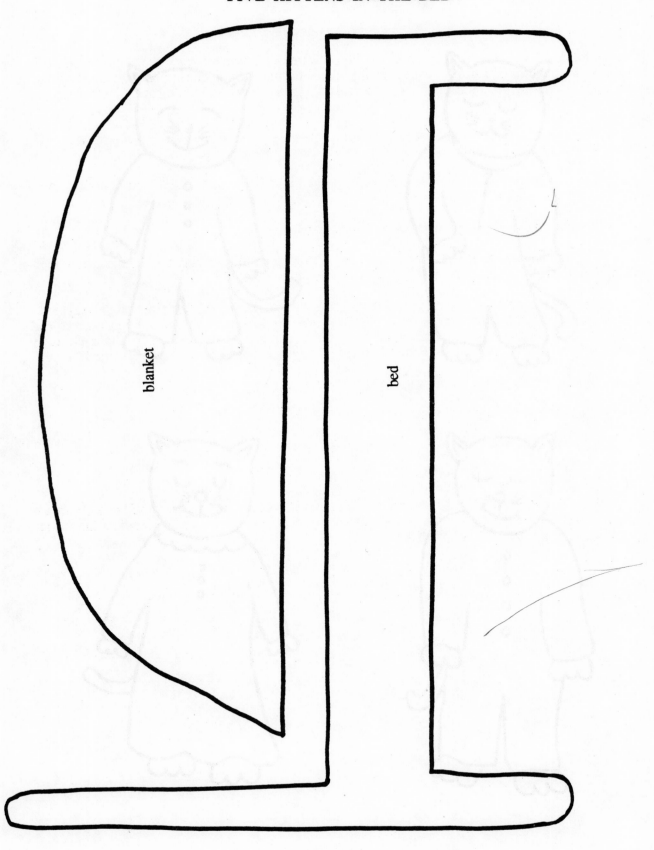

blanket

bed

THE LION AND THE MOUSE

(A Fable from Aesop)

One day a lion was resting under his favorite tree. He was sitting there so still that a tiny mouse didn't even notice him. Not knowing where he was going, the mouse ran up the lion's body right to the top of his head. The lion roared! In an angry voice he said, "How dare you disturb the king of the beasts!"

The mouse was so scared he was shaking. "Please don't hurt me lion," cried the mouse. "Please let me go and I promise that someday I will repay your kindness."

The lion roared with laughter and said, "What could a tiny fellow like you ever do to help me?"

"I don't know. But someday I will," said the mouse.

The lion decided to let the mouse go free. Although he didn't believe what the mouse said, he did think the mouse was quite funny.

Not much time passed and the lion found himself caught in a hunter's net. He struggled to get free and let out a great roar. Far away in the jungle the little mouse heard the lion's roar and came running as fast as his little feet could carry him. The mouse found the lion and right away started to chew the rope that held the net together. The net fell open and the lion was free!

"Thank you so much for saving my life!" said the lion.

"I was happy to help you," replied the mouse.

From that time on, the lion and the mouse became the best of friends.

Directions

Make a small net by tying together a few pieces of white yarn (yarn will stick easily to felt or flannel). Place the "net" over the lion at the appropriate time. Remove the net after the mouse "chews" it. Use the tree pattern on pages 130 - 131.

THE LION AND THE MOUSE

FIVE LITTLE PIGS

(Folk Rhyme)

The first little pig
danced a merry, merry jig.
The second little pig ate candy.
The third little pig
Wore a blue and yellow wig.
The fourth little pig was dandy.
The fifth little pig
Never grew very big,
And they called him
Tiny Little Andy.

Directions

Place the pigs on the flannel board in succession as they appear in the rhyme.

FIVE LITTLE PIGS

FIDDLE-I-FEE

(For melody and extra verses see Music Appendix, Song 10)

I had a cat and the cat pleased me,
I fed my cat under yonder tree.
Cat goes fiddle-i-fee.

I had a hen...
I had a duck...
I had a sheep...
I had a pig...
I had a horse...
I had a cow...

Directions

Add the animals to the flannel board in succession according to the song. Be sure to keep them in order on the flannel board. This will help you remember what comes next in the song.

126

FIDDLE-I-FEE

FIDDLE-I-FEE

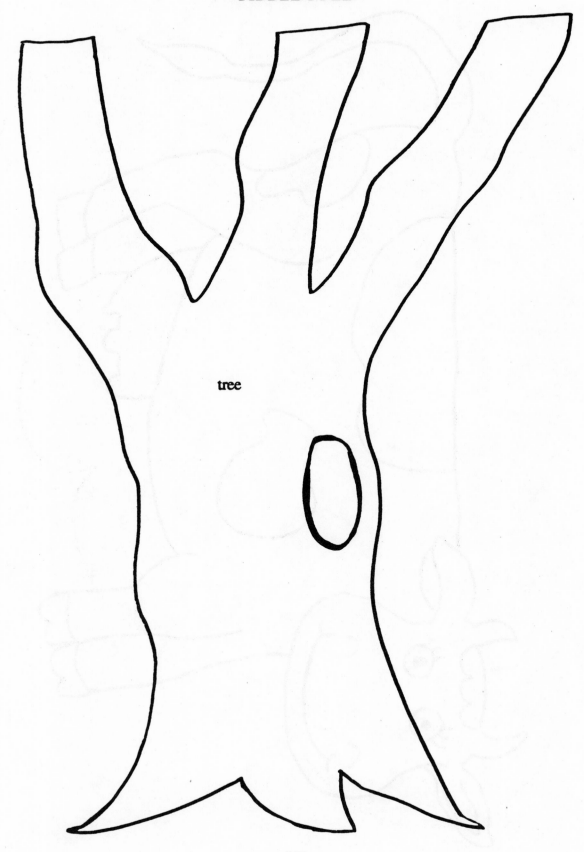

tree

FIDDLE-I-FEE

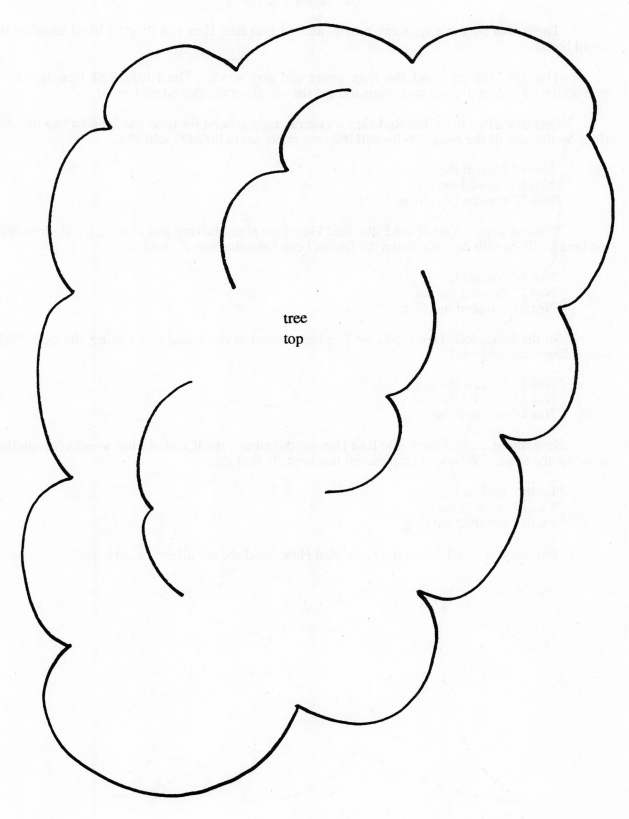

tree
top

THE LITTLE RED HEN

(An English Folk Tale)

There was once a dog, a cat, a frog, and a Little Red Hen and they all lived together in a small house.

The dog, the cat, and the frog never did any work. The Little Red Hen had to do everything. She had to cook and clean and get the wood for the fire all by herself.

One day when the Little Red Hen was scratching around for food she found a bag of wheat flour by the side of the road. "Who will help me make some bread?" said she.

"Not I," barked the dog.
"Not I," mewed the cat.
"Not I," croaked the frog.

Without saying a word the Little Red Hen went about mixing and stirring the flour to make the bread. "Who will help me make the fire so I can bake the bread?" said she.

"Not I," barked the dog.
"Not I," mewed the cat.
"Not I," croaked the frog.

So the Little Red Hen made the fire herself and as the bread was baking she said, "Who will help me set the table?"

"Not I," barked the dog.
"Not I," mewed the cat.
"Not I," croaked the frog.

So without a word the Little Red Hen set the table herself and put the wonderful smelling bread on the table. "Who will help me eat this bread?" said she.

"I will!" barked the dog.
"I will!" mewed the cat.
"I will!" croaked the frog.

"Oh, no you won't!" said the Little Red Hen. And she ate all the bread herself.

Place the table on the flannel board when the Little Red Hen begins to make the bread. Put the loaf of bread over the fire at the appropriate time. When she sets the table, place the bread on the table.

FIVE LITTLE COOKIES

(Folk Rhyme Adapted by Diane Briggs)

Five little cookies in a bakery shop,
Shining bright with sugar on top.
Along came a girl (or boy) with a penny one day,
And bought a cookie and ran away.

Four little cookies...
Three little cookies...
Two little cookies...
One little cookie...

Directions

Count the five cookies as you place them on the flannel board. As you say the poem, remove one cookie each verse.

WHERE'S MY DADDY

(by Diane Briggs)

A little dinosaur with a long neck was lost in the forest. He was looking for his daddy. He walked and walked until he came upon a big orange dinosaur.

"Have you seen my Daddy?" asked the little dinosaur.

"Is he big and orange with a large duck bill like me?" said the orange dinosaur.

"No, he isn't orange and he doesn't have a duck bill either," replied the little dinosaur.

"Then I'm sorry, I haven't seen him," said the orange dinosaur and he plodded off into the forest.

The little dinosaur walked on and on until he met a brown dinosaur with spikes on his back and tail.

"Have you seen my Daddy?" asked the little dinosaur.

"Does he have spikes on his back and a long tail with spikes on the end?" asked the brown dinosaur.

"No, he has a long tail but no spikes," replied the little dinosaur.

"Sorry, I haven't seen him then," said the brown dinosaur and he went back into the forest.

And the little dinosaur walked on and on looking for his daddy. Soon he came upon a giant blue dinosaur with long sharp teeth. The little dinosaur was scared but he asked in a shaky voice, "Have you seen my Daddy?"

"Roar! No, I haven't!" said the giant dinosaur and he bounded off into the forest.

The little dinosaur was glad the blue dinosaur was gone and he walked on. Soon he saw a flying dinosaur with purple wings and asked, "Have you seen my Daddy?"

The flying dinosaur replied, "I thought I saw a long-necked dinosaur a little farther on into the forest." "Goodbye," he said as he flew away.

The little dinosaur ran in the direction the flying dinosaur had told him. After a while he heard some sounds in the forest. He hoped it wasn't the giant blue dinosaur. He went a little further and there was his Daddy!

"Daddy, where have you been? I've been looking all over for you!" And his Daddy gave him a big hug.

Directions

Place the dinosaurs on the flannel board as they appear in the story. Remove them when they go back into the forest.

WHERE'S MY DADDY

WHERE'S MY DADDY

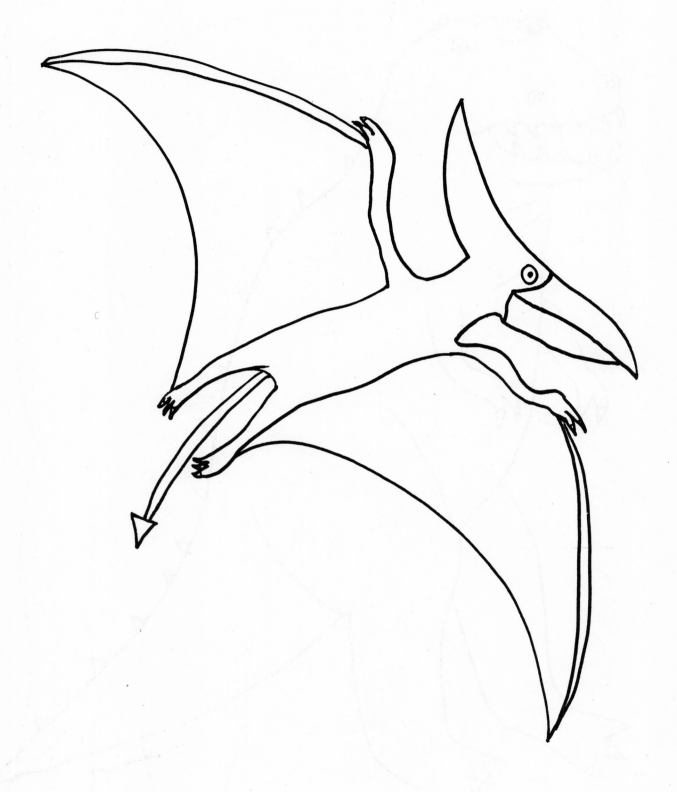

WHERE'S MY DADDY

GETTING DRESSED

(by Diane Briggs)

I have a funny hat,
And a shirt that's green and blue.
I have some yellow pants,
And some boots that are brand new.

What else should I wear?
Oh! Look at it snow!
I better put on my snowsuit,
'Cause it's forty-two below!

Directions

Put the clothes on the child as you say the poem. A small piece of tape or Velcro placed on the back of the child will help insure that nothing falls off the flannel board.

GETTING DRESSED

FUZZY, WUZZY CATERPILLAR

(Author Unknown)

Fuzzy Wuzzy caterpillar,
Into a corner will creep.
He'll spin himself a blanket,
And then fall fast asleep.

Fuzzy Wuzzy caterpillar,
Wakes up by and by.
To find his wings of beauty,
Changed to a butterfly!

Directions

Place the caterpillar on the flannel board and cover him with the chrysalis when you say the line: "He'll spin himself a blanket." Remove these pieces and replace them with the butterfly at the end of the poem.

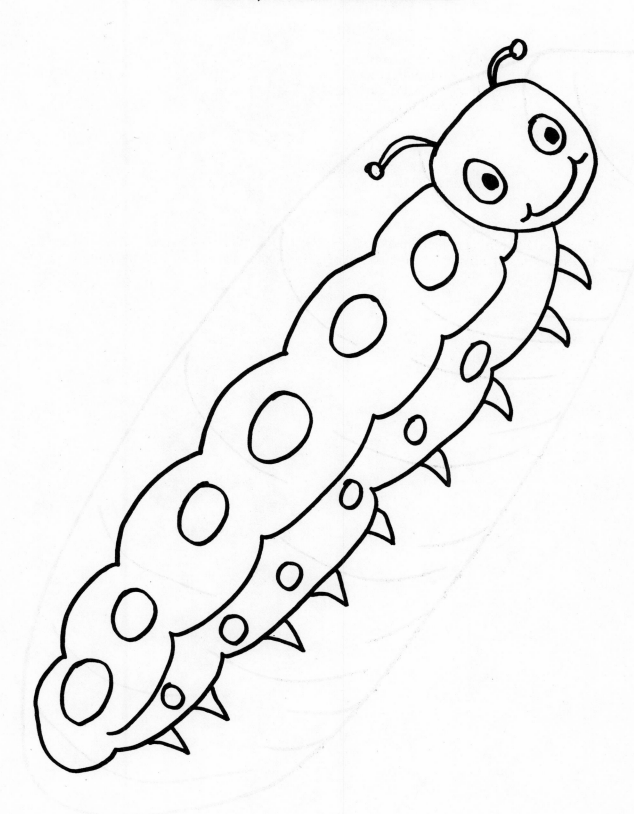

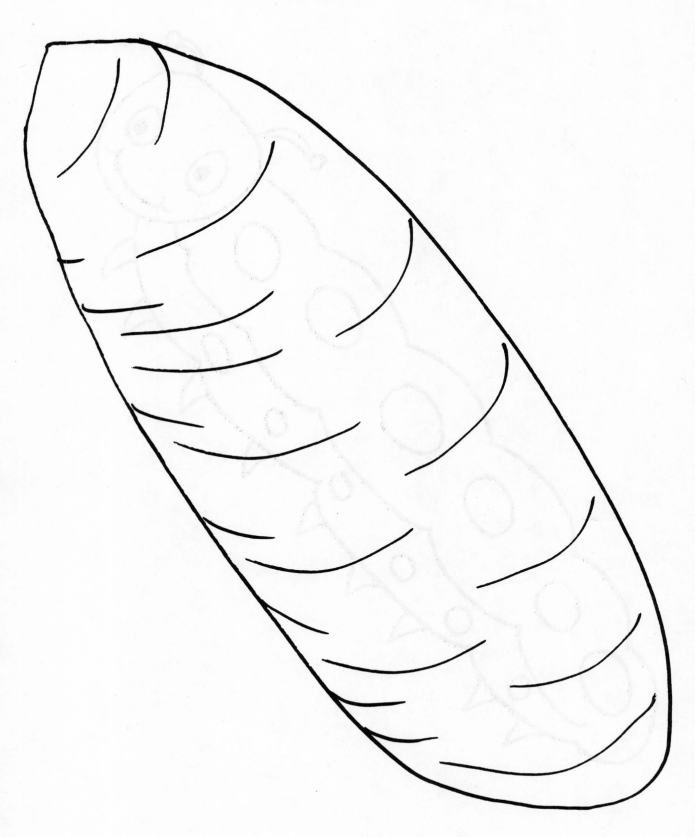

FUZZY, WUZZY CATERPILLAR

FIVE LITTLE PUMPKINS

(Folk Rhyme)

Five little pumpkins sitting on a gate,
First one said, "Oh, my, it's getting late."
Second one said, "There's witches in the air."
Third one said, "I don't care."
Fourth one said, "Let's run and run and run."
Fifth one said, "I'm ready for some fun."
So, Ooooooo went the wind,
And out went the light,
And the five little pumpkins,
Rolled out of sight!

Directions

Make a gate with strips of white felt. Place the pumpkins on the flannel board one by one as you recite the rhyme. Remove them at the end of the rhyme.

FIVE LITTLE SNOWPEOPLE

(Author Unknown)

Five little snowpeople knocking at my door,
One melts away, then there are four.
Four little snowpeople playing with me,
One melts away, then there are three.
Three little snowpeople playing with you,
One melts away, then there are two.
Two little snowpeople playing in the sun,
One melts away, then there is one.
One little snowperson when the day is done,
Just melts away, then there is none.

Directions

Before beginning the rhyme, place the snowpeople on the flannel board. Remove them one by one as they melt away.

FIVE LITTLE SNOWPEOPLE

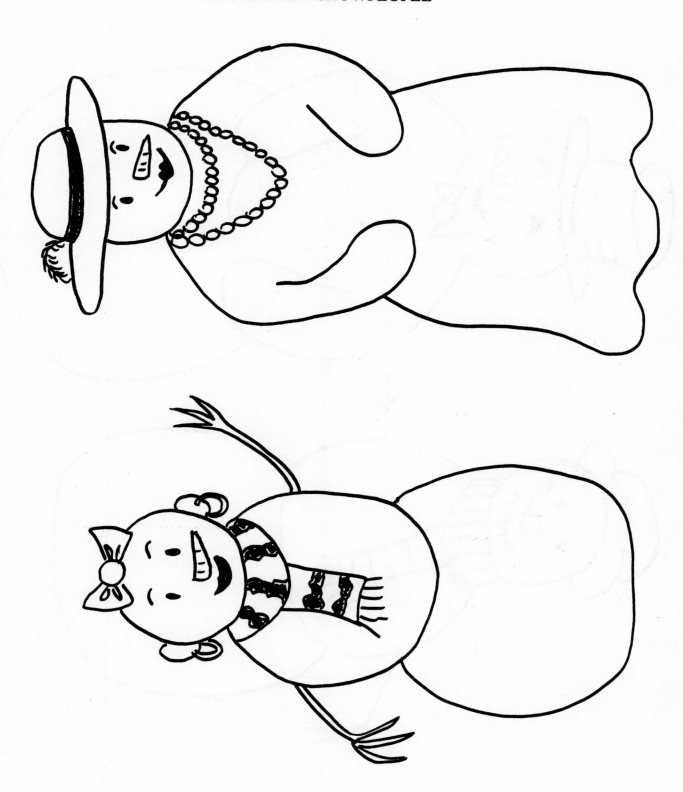

FIVE LITTLE SNOWPEOPLE

HUSH LITTLE BABY

(For melody see Music Appendix, Song 25)

Hush little baby, don't say a word,
Mama's gonna buy you a mocking bird.

If that mocking bird don't sing,
Mama's gonna buy you a diamond ring.

If that diamond ring turns brass,
Mama's gonna buy you a looking glass.

If that looking glass gets broke,
Mama's gonna buy you a billy goat.

If that billy goat don't pull,
Mama's gonna buy you a cart and bull.

If that cart and bull turn over,
Mama's gonna buy you a dog named Rover.

If that dog named Rover don't bark,
Mama's gonna buy you a horse and cart.

If that horse and cart fall down,
You'll still be the sweetest little baby in town.

Directions

Place the baby on the center of the flannel board. Put all the objects and animals on the flannel board in succession as you sing the song.

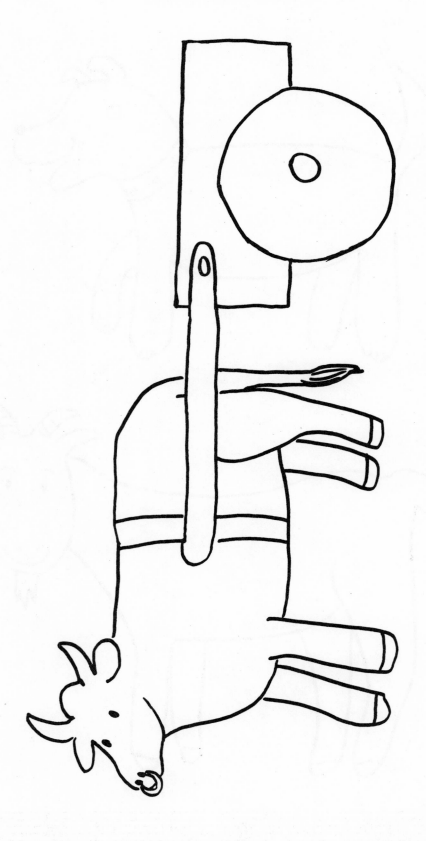

MUSIC APPENDIX

SONGS LISTED BY NUMBER

1. All the Fish are Swimming in the Water
2. Little Rabbit Foo-Foo
3. Head, Shoulders, Knees, and Toes
4. Rub-A-Dub-Dub
5. Five Brown Teddies
6. Lavender's Blue
7. Down by the Station
8. Little Miss Muffet
9. Down on Grandpa's Farm
10. Fiddle-I-Fee
11. Mr. Sun
12. Glack Goon
13. Five Little Ducks
14. Rags
15. Monkey See, Monkey Do
16. The Oink Song
17. Hickory Dickory Dock
18. The Animal Fair
19. I Had a Little Rooster
20. Peanut Butter and Jelly
21. Mary Wore A Red Dress
22. Baby Bumble Bee
23. If You're Happy
24. Bluebird
25. Hush Little Baby

1. All the Fish Are
Swimming in the Water

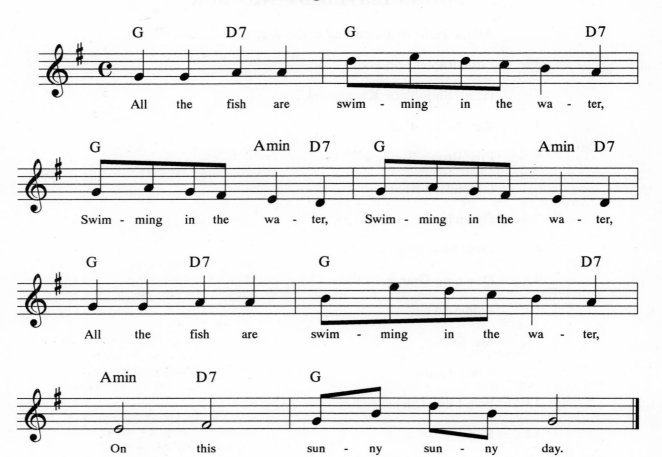

All the fish are swim - ming in the wa - ter,

Swim - ming in the wa - ter, Swim - ming in the wa - ter,

All the fish are swim - ming in the wa - ter,

On this sun - ny sun - ny day.

162

2. Little Rabbit Foo-Foo

(spoken)   Down came the Good Fairy,
And she said— (to verse 2)

(spoken)   "I'll give you three chances,
And if you don't behave,
I'll turn you into a goon."
The next day— (to verse 3)

3.   Little Rabbit Foo-Foo,
Hopping through the forest,
Scooping up the field mice,
And bopping them on the head.

(spoken)   Down came the Good Fairy,
And she said— (to verse 4)

4.   Little Rabbit Foo-Foo,
I don't like your attitude,
Scooping up the field mice,
And bopping them on the head.

(spoken)   "I'll give you two chances,
And if you don't behave,
I'll turn you into a goon."
The next day— (to verse 5)

5.   Little Rabbit Foo-Foo,
Hopping through the forest,
Scooping up the field mice,
And bopping them on the head.

(spoken)   Down came the Good Fairy,
And she said— (to verse 6)

6.   Little Rabbit Foo-Foo,
I don't like your attitude,
Scooping up the field mice,
And bopping them on the head.

(spoken)   "I'll give you one more chance,
And if you don't behave,
I'll turn you into a goon."
The next day— (to verse 7)

7.   Little Rabbit Foo-Foo,
Hopping through the forest,
Scooping up the field mice,
And bopping them on the head.

(spoken)   Down came the Good Fairy,
And she said— (to verse 8)

8.   Little Rabbit Foo-Foo,
I don't like your attitude,
Scooping up the field mice,
And bopping them on the head.

(spoken)   "I gave you three chances,
And you didn't behave.
Now, I'll turn you into a goon."
POOF!!!

The moral of the story is:

HARE TODAY, GOON TOMORROW!!

3. Head, Shoulders, Knees, and Toes

Head and should - ers, knees and toes, knees and toes,

Head and should - ers, knees and toes, knees and toes,_____ and_____

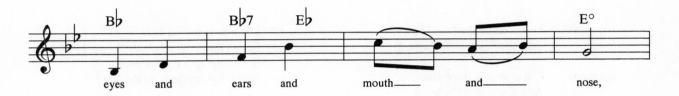

eyes and ears and mouth_____ and_____ nose,

Head and should - ers, knees and toes, knees and toes.

4. Rub-A-Dub-Dub

Rub - a - dub - dub, three men in a tub, And who do you think they be?_____ The

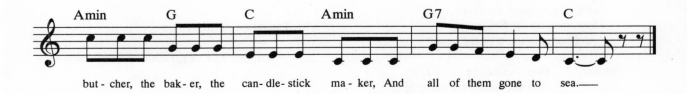

but - cher, the bak - er, the can - dle - stick ma - ker, And all of them gone to sea._____

5. Five Brown Teddies

Five   brown   ted - dies   sit - ting   on   a   wall,
Four   brown   ted - dies   sit - ting   on   a   wall,
Three   brown   ted - dies   sit - ting   on   a   wall,
Two   brown   ted - dies   sit - ting   on   a   wall,
One   brown   ted - dy   sit - ting   on   a   wall,

Five   brown   ted - dies   sit - ting   on   a   wall.
Four   brown   ted - dies   sit - ting   on   a   wall.
Three   brown   ted - dies   sit - ting   on   a   wall.
Two   brown   ted - dies   sit - ting   on   a   wall.
One   brown   ted - dy   sit - ting   on   a   wall.

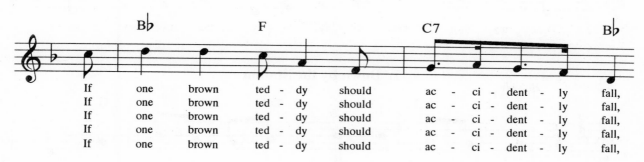

If   one   brown   ted - dy   should   ac - ci - dent - ly   fall,
If   one   brown   ted - dy   should   ac - ci - dent - ly   fall,
If   one   brown   ted - dy   should   ac - ci - dent - ly   fall,
If   one   brown   ted - dy   should   ac - ci - dent - ly   fall,
If   one   brown   ted - dy   should   ac - ci - dent - ly   fall,

There'd be   four   brown   ted - dies   sit - ting   on   a   wall.
There'd be   three brown   ted - dies   sit - ting   on   a   wall.
There'd be   two   brown   ted - dies   sit - ting   on   a   wall.
There'd be   one   brown   ted - dies   sit - ting   on   a   wall.
There'd be   no   brown   ted - dies   sit - ting   on   a   wall.

6. Lavender's Blue

Lightly

La - ven - der's blue, dil - ly, dil - ly, la - ven - der's green;

When I am King, dil - ly, dil - ly, you shall be Queen.

Who told you so, dil - ly, dil - ly, who told you so?

'Twas my own heart, dil - ly, dil - ly, that told me so.

7. Down by the Station

Briskly

Down by the sta - tion, ear - ly in the morn - ing,

See the lit - tle puff - er bel - lies all in a row;

See the en - gine dri - ver pull the lit - tle han - dle,

Chug, Chug, Puff, Puff! Off we go!

8. Little Miss Muffet

Lit-tle Miss Muf-fet sat on a tuf-fet, Eat-ing her curds and whey;—— A-

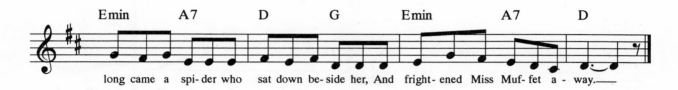

long came a spi-der who sat down be-side her, And fright-ened Miss Muf-fet a - way.——

9. Down on Grandpa's Farm

Oh we're on our way, we're on our way, on our way to Grand-pa's farm.

We're on our way, We're on our way, on our way to Grand-pa's farm. farm.

Verses

Down on grand-pa's farm there is a big brown cow. Down on grand-pa's

farm there is a big brown cow. The cow, she makes a sound like

this: Moo! Moo! The cow, she makes a sound like this: Moo! Moo!

2. little red hen. 3. little white sheep. 4. big black dog. 5. big brown horse.

10. Fiddle-I-Fee

Have fun

1. I had a cat and the cat pleased me, I fed my cat un - der

yon - der tree. Cat goes fid - dle - i - fee. 2. I had a hen and the
3. I had a duck and the

Repeat in reverse

hen pleased me, I fed my hen un - der yon - der tree. Hen goes chim- my chuck, chim- my chuck.
duck pleased me, I fed my duck un - der yon - der tree. Duck goes qua— - ck, qua— - ck.

2. Cat goes fid - dle - i - fee. **D.S.** I

3. Cat goes fid - dle - i - fee.

4. I had a sheep and the sheep pleased me,
   I fed my sheep under yonder tree.
   Sheep goes baa, baa,
   Duck goes quack, quack,
   Hen goes chimmy chuck, chimmy chuck,
   Cat goes fiddle-i-fee.

5. I had a pig and the pig pleased me,
   I fed my pig under yonder tree.
   Pig goes oink, oink,
   Sheep goes baa, baa,
   Duck goes quack, quack,
   Hen goes chimmy chuck, chimmy chuck,
   Cat goes fiddle-i-fee.

6. I had a horse and the horse pleased me,
   I fed my horse under yonder tree.
   Horse goes neigh, neigh,
   Pig goes oink, oink,
   Sheep goes baa, baa,
   Duck goes quack, quack,
   Hen goes chimmy chuck, chimmy chuck,
   Cat goes fiddle-i-fee.

7. I had a cow and the cow pleased me,
   I fed my cow under yonder tree.
   Cow goes moo, moo,
   Horse goes neigh, neigh,
   Pig goes oink, oink,
   Sheep goes baa, baa,
   Duck goes quack, quack,
   Hen goes chimmy chuck, chimmy chuck,
   Cat goes fiddle-i-fee.

11. Mr. Sun

Medium fast

Oh Mis- ter Sun, Sun, Mis- ter Gol- den Sun, please shine down on

me. Oh Mis- ter Sun, Sun, Mis- ter Gol- den Sun, hi- ding be- hind a tree.

These lit- tle chil- dren are— ask- ing you to please come out so we can

play with you. Oh Mis- ter Sun, Sun, Mis- ter Gol- den Sun, please shine down on me.

12. Glack Goon

Glack Goon went the lit- tle green frog one day, Glack Goon went the lit- tle green

frog one day, Glack Goon went the lit- tle green frog one day, And his eyes went glack glack goon.

13. Five Little Ducks

Brightly

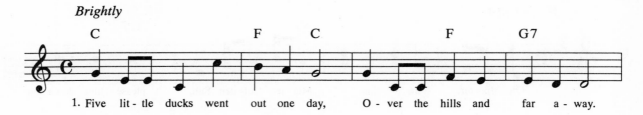

1. Five lit-tle ducks went out one day, O-ver the hills and far a-way.

Mo-ther duck said, "Quack, quack, quack, quack!" But on-ly four lit-tle ducks came back.

2. Four little ducks went out one day...
   But only three little ducks came back.

3. Three little ducks went out one day...
   But only two little ducks came back.

4. Two little ducks went out one day...
   But only one little duck came back.

5. One little duck went out one day...
   But none of the five little ducks came back.

6. Sad mother duck went out one day...
   And all of the five little ducks came back.

14. Rags

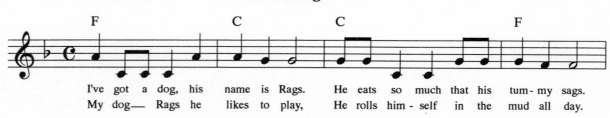

I've got a dog, his name is Rags. He eats so much that his tum-my sags.
My dog— Rags he likes to play, He rolls him-self in the mud all day.

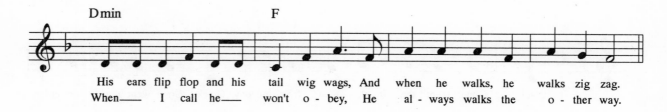

His ears flip flop and his tail wig wags, And when he walks, he walks zig zag.
When— I call he— won't o-bey, He al-ways walks the o-ther way.

Repeat 3X

He goes flip flop wig wag zig zag, I love Rags and he loves me.

15. Monkey See, Monkey Do

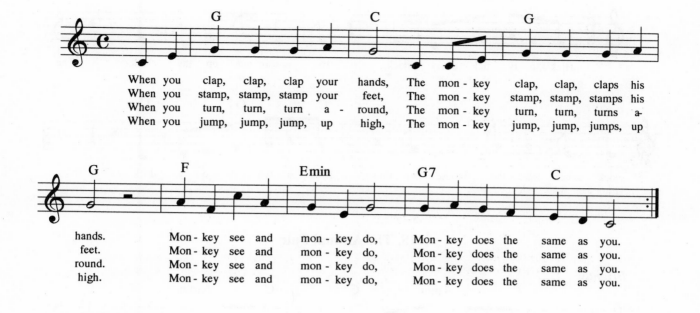

When you clap, clap, clap your hands, The mon-key clap, clap, claps his
When you stamp, stamp, stamp your feet, The mon-key stamp, stamp, stamps his
When you turn, turn, turn a - round, The mon-key turn, turn, turns a-
When you jump, jump, jump, up high, The mon-key jump, jump, jumps, up

hands. Mon - key see and mon - key do, Mon - key does the same as you.
feet. Mon - key see and mon - key do, Mon - key does the same as you.
round. Mon - key see and mon - key do, Mon - key does the same as you.
high. Mon - key see and mon - key do, Mon - key does the same as you.

16. The Oink Song

There was an old wo-man and she had a lit-tle pig,— oink, oink, oink. There

was an old wo-man and she had a lit-tle pig. It did - n't eat much 'cause it

was - n't ve - ry big,— oink, oink, oink.

17. Hickory Dickory Dock

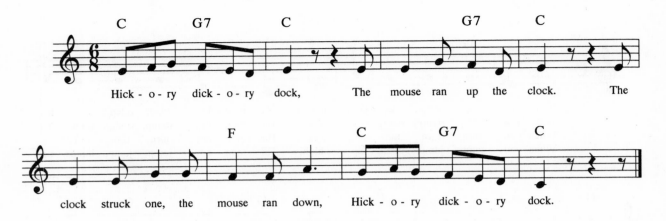

Hick - o - ry dick - o - ry dock, The mouse ran up the clock. The
clock struck one, the mouse ran down, Hick - o - ry dick - o - ry dock.

18. The Animal Fair

I went to the a - ni - mal fair.__ The birds and the beasts were there.__ The
big ba - boon by the light of the moon Was comb - ing his or - ange hair,__ The
mon - key bumped the skunk.__ And climbed up the e - le - phant's trunk;__ The
e - le - phant sneezed and fell to his knees, And that was the end of the monk, the monk, the
monk, the monk. The monk. The monk. The monk.

19. I Had a Little Rooster

With good humor

I had a lit-tle roos-ter by the barn-yard gate, And that lit-tle roos-ter was

my play-mate. And that lit-tle roos-ter sang: Cock - a - doo-dle - doo,

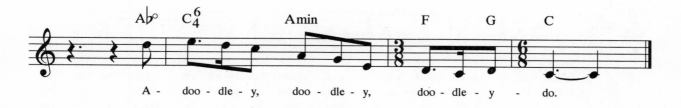

A - doo - dle - y, doo - dle - y, doo - dle - y - do.

2. I had a little hen by the barnyard gate,
And that little hen was my playmate,
And that little hen sang: Cluck, cluck, cluck,
And that little rooster sang: Cock-a-doo-dle-doo,
A doodley, doodley, doodley-doo.

3. I had a little cow by the barnyard gate,
And that little cow was my playmate,
And that little cow sang: Moo, moo,
And that little hen sang: Cluck, cluck, cluck,
And that little rooster sang: Cock-a-doo-dle-doo,
A doodley, doodley, doodley-doo.

4. I had a little dog by the barnyard gate,
And that little dog was my playmate,
And that little dog sang: Woof, woof, woof,
And that little cow sang: Moo, moo,
And that little hen sang: Cluck, cluck, cluck,
And that little rooster sang: Cock-a-doo-dle-doo,
A doodley, doodley, doodley-doo.

20. Peanut Butter and Jelly

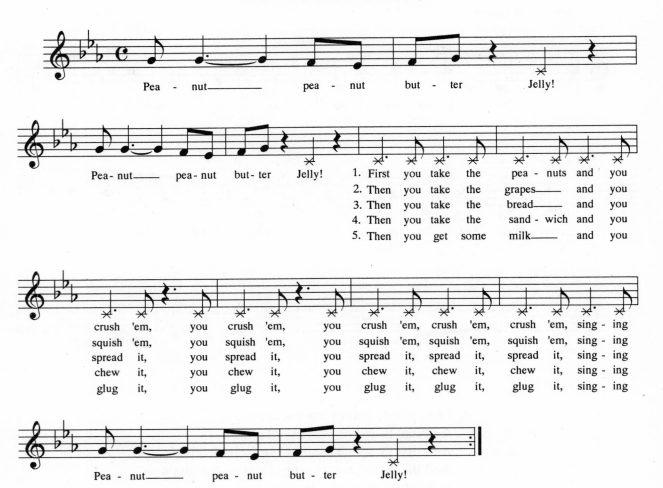

Pea - nut_____ pea - nut but - ter Jelly!

Pea - nut_____ pea - nut but - ter Jelly!

1. First you take the pea - nuts and you
2. Then you take the grapes_____ and you
3. Then you take the bread_____ and you
4. Then you take the sand - wich and you
5. Then you get some milk_____ and you

crush 'em, you crush 'em, you crush 'em, crush 'em, crush 'em, sing - ing
squish 'em, you squish 'em, you squish 'em, squish 'em, squish 'em, sing - ing
spread it, you spread it, you spread it, spread it, spread it, sing - ing
chew it, you chew it, you chew it, chew it, chew it, sing - ing
glug it, you glug it, you glug it, glug it, glug it, sing - ing

Pea - nut_____ pea - nut but - ter Jelly!

21. Mary Wore a Red Dress

Simply

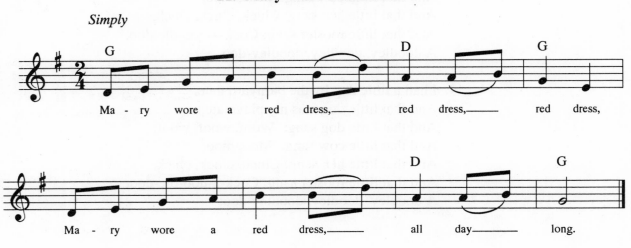

Ma - ry wore a red dress,_____ red dress,_____ red dress,

Ma - ry wore a red dress,_____ all day_____ long.

22. Baby Bumble Bee

Oh, I'm bring - ing home a ba - by bum - ble bee,

Won't my mom - my be so proud of me, 'Cause I'm

bring - ing home a ba - by bum - ble bee. Buz - zy, buz - zy, buz - zy OOH, he stung me!
(spoken)

23. If You're Happy

If you're hap - py and you know it, clap your hands *(clap, clap)*. If you're

hap - py and you know it, clap your hands *(clap, clap)*. If you're hap - py and you know it, then you

real - ly ought to show it. If you're hap - py and you know it, clap your hands *(clap, clap)*.

24. Bluebird

Blue-bird, blue — -bird, Through — my — win - dow, Blue-bird, blue — -bird,
Take a lit - tle girl, tap her on the shoul - der, Take a lit - tle girl,

Through — my — win - dow, Blue-bird, blue — -bird, Through — my — win - dow,
tap her on the shoul - der, Take a lit - tle girl, tap her on the shoul - der,

Oh, mom - my I'm so tir - ed.
Oh, mom - my I'm so tir - ed.

25. Hush Little Baby

1. Hush lit - tle ba - by, don't say a word,
2. If that___ mock - ing bird don't___ sing,
3. If that___ dia - mond ring turns___ brass,
4. If that___ look - ing glass gets___ broke,
5. If that___ bil - ly goat don't___ pull,
6. If that___ cart and bull turn___ over,
7. If that___ dog named Rover don't___ bark,
8. If that___ horse and cart fall___ down,

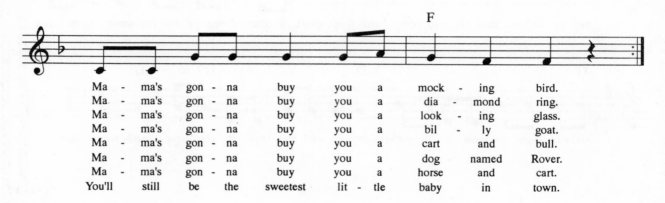

Ma - ma's gon - na buy you a mock - ing bird.
Ma - ma's gon - na buy you a dia - mond ring.
Ma - ma's gon - na buy you a look - ing glass.
Ma - ma's gon - na buy you a bil - ly goat.
Ma - ma's gon - na buy you a cart and bull.
Ma - ma's gon - na buy you a dog named Rover.
Ma - ma's gon - na buy you a horse and cart.
You'll still be the sweetest lit - tle baby in town.

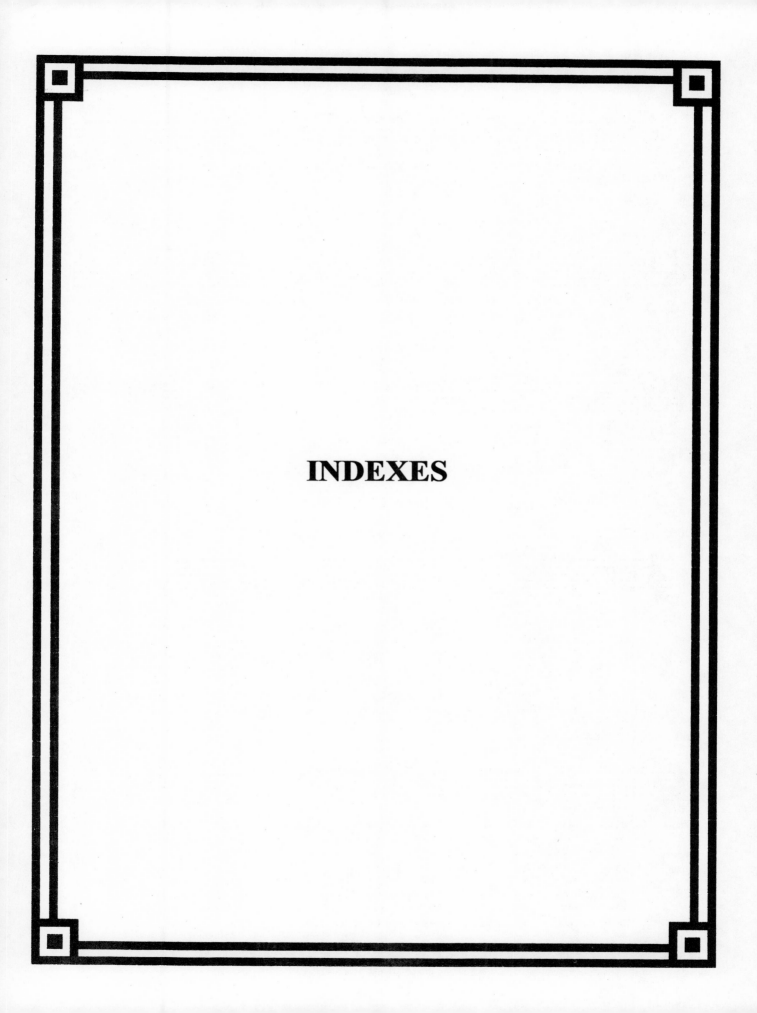

INDEXES

INDEX TO AUTHORS AND TITLES

INDEX TO FINGERPLAYS AND ACTION RHYMES

Many of the fingerplays and action rhymes included in this book are traditional rhymes and are of unknown origin unless otherwise indicated in the text.

ABOUT THE AUTHOR

Diane Briggs is an elementary school librarian at the Maplewood School in Watervliet, New York. Previously a children's librarian at the Bethlehem Public Library in Delmar, New York, she holds an M.L.S. from the State University of New York at Albany.

During the course of her work as a children's librarian and storyteller, Briggs has worked extensively in toddler programming. The enthusiastic response of children in her storytime programs has been the inspiration for this book. She is also the author of *Flannel Board Fun: A Collection of Stories, Songs, and Poems* (Scarecrow, 1992).

Ms. Briggs lives in Delmar with her husband Scott and six-year-old son Thomas.